P9-DGV-716

DISCIPLINE
THAT WORKS

5 SIMPLE STEPS

JOYCE DIVINYI, M.S., L.P.C.

The Wellness Connection

Discipline That Works: 5 Simple Steps

is published by The Wellness Connection.

Copyright © 2003 by The Wellness Connection.
All rights reserved. Printed in the United States of America.
No part of this book may be used or
reproduced or transmitted in any form by any means
without written permission except in the case of
reprints in the context of reviews.

The above symbol is a trademark of the Wellness Connection
and is copyright protected.

Attention Schools & Businesses:
This book is available at quantity discounts with bulk purchase
for educational, business, or sales promotional use.
For information, write to
Special Sales Department
The Wellness Connection
125 Highgreen Ridge
Peachtree City, GA 30269
Phone: 770-631-8264 Toll Free: 888-460-8022
Fax: 770-486-1609
Website: www.thehumanconnection.net
Email address: joyce@thehumanconnection.net

ISBN: 0-9656353-7-6

Final editing, page design/layout & cover design by
Connie L. Schmidt & Ron Kaye
Schmidt Kaye & Company Professional Literary Services
Houston, Texas

For Elizabeth Fallon
*With heartfelt gratitude for her enduring friendship
and loving encouragement.*

Acknowledgements

I wish to express my sincere gratitude and appreciation to the treasured friends, family and colleagues who have helped bring this book to fruition. Tammy Bjugson has worked side by side with me for many years and without her care, concern and attention to detail I would be lost. Betty Shaw continues to nudge and prod when I get off-task, which is all too often. Cathie Coppedge is relentless when researching via the Internet and her help is always greatly appreciated. Mitch Davis is the personification of loving patience when it comes to all things technical, an area in which I am hopeless.

Sandy Halperin has been a healer and a mentor and has taught me many things besides the Two Sentence Rule. These kind people never cease to amaze me and are God's gift of grace to my life. I also want to thank my daughters Bridy and Erin and my sisters Norma and Marilynn for being endlessly supportive and encouraging. Of all of the blessings in my life they are the most precious.

Most of all, I want to thank my dear friend and editor Jerry Spurgeon for his never-ending patience and good humor. Even when we argued about sentence structure or syntax, he was always fun and pleasant, all the while refusing to yield his point. This book would not have happened without his good work.

- *Joyce Divinyi*

TABLE OF CONTENTS

INTRODUCTION

Children and teens can and do bring great joy to the lives of the adults around them. They are especially enjoyable when they are happy and well behaved. They are usually happy and essentially well behaved when they are loved, nurtured and well disciplined. But sometimes trying to get children or teens to behave properly can seem like the most overwhelming job on the planet. Teaching them to respond respectfully to adult directions, to control their own behavior, and to make good choices is the most challenging and important task an adult can undertake. These tasks demand commitment, skills and a few good ideas.

Discipline That Works: 5 Simple Steps offers an uncommon but highly effective approach to helping children learn the things they need to know to be successful and happy in life. The *5 Simple Steps* are about effective discipline. Good and appropriate discipline is meant to teach. In fact, the meaning of discipline is "to teach." One problem, however, is that discipline often does not get the desired results. This is because discipline often gets confused with punishment. Punishment, as I will discuss, is not the same thing as discipline, nor is it a substitute for discipline.

It is a common mistake to confuse punishment with discipline. Punishment is meant to make children sorry for misbehaving. Discipline, here, means teaching children to develop and use self-control and good judgment by teaching them skills. If it does not teach, it is not discipline. Punishment, on the other hand, is based on the belief that if children suffer for their mistakes they won't make them again. We assume that paying for mistakes usually helps people think twice before they make the same mistake again. We also tend to assume that all behavior is about thinking. We believe that everyone, including children, is always thinking about what they are doing before, during and after they do it. This is not necessarily true.

A great deal of human behavior is prompted by emotions, rather than the act of thinking. This creates a problem when it comes to punishing children for mistakes. Three things have to happen for punishment to change behavior. First, the person has to be aware of the *feelings* that are prompting them to break the rules. Second, they have to be able to *think* about what they are about to do and what might happen if they do it. And third, and most importantly, they have to be able to figure out how to keep themselves from *acting* solely on their feelings. If they are not able to do these three things, in this order, punishment is not likely to have much effect.

This simple sequence of events that takes place in the brain is taken for granted by most mature adults. They have learned how to process these three things in an automatic fashion. Their brains move through this sequence quite readily. An example would be the situation on those mornings when the alarm goes off and the urge (a feeling) to turn it off and go to sleep again is quite powerful. Then a little voice in your head (your thinking brain) activates, and you start considering the consequences of just not showing up for work... things like getting fired, not being able to make your house and car payments, and so on. Then you have a short dialogue with yourself, and the next thing you know, you take action. You get up, take a shower, and are off to work.

The *Emotions-Thinking-Action*, or E-T-A, sequence of events doesn't sound so complicated, but it does require the brain to move from the *feeling* mode, to the *thinking* mode, and on to the *action* mode rather quickly. This sequence doesn't always happen for children and teens. Children's brains are not fully developed. They have not yet learned the skills necessary for talking themselves into doing the right thing. Instead, they just continue doing what they feel like doing at the moment.

When the E-T-A sequence gets mixed up, the result can be that *feelings* end up driving behavior. A *feeling* happens and, Bingo!...an *action* follows immediately. There are even some adults that haven't yet mastered the skill of talking (*thinking*) themselves out of *acting* on an impulse. We all get this sequence out of order from time to time. We act on *feelings* instead of good *thinking* skills. With children, the *Emotion* to *Action* sequence happens quite often. This prompts adults to ask the age-old question, "What were you *thinking*?!" The answer to that question is usually, "I don't know." Then adults become frustrated. They cannot believe that anyone, even a young person, does not know what they are thinking. What causes this frustrating situation to occur? The answer lies in the way in which the brain is organized.

Brain function is the key. The brain is a compartmentalized organ; different parts of the brain do different jobs. The part of the brain that makes it possible to *feel* and experience emotions is different from the part that enables us to *think*. The ability to think about things that could happen in the future (consequences) requires that both the *feeling* and *thinking* parts of the brain are able to communicate with each other. Sometimes this brain communication gets off track. This frequently happens with young children and teens. Adults then have to "save youth from themselves." As children mature, their brain makes more and more trips from *feeling* to *thinking* and then onward to consideration of future consequences. Eventually neuro-pathways are developed and fewer and fewer *action*s happen strictly on impulse.

There are numerous things that can interfere with the development of these neuro-pathways and can result in the child becoming more unrestrained in his behavior. Sometimes this interference comes from circumstances in the child's life. Sometimes it is a matter of neuro-chemicals that are not working properly. Most frequently, it is a matter of inadequate supervision and training where the child has not been adequately taught to reflect on his or her behavior. When children are left too much on their own, or have not been taught how to behave appropriately, their brains do not adequately develop the ability to move through the proper sequence of *Emotions* (E), *Thinking* (T) and *Action* (A).

The E-T-A Sequence

Effective discipline helps children develop the E-T-A sequence in their brains. Punishment alone does not necessarily have the same effect. Punishment does cause suffering, and on occasion will work for a short-term result. However, punishment doesn't necessarily ensure that the proper E-T-A sequence will happen in the brain the next time the same or a similar situation comes up. This is where the *5 Simple Steps* provide an effective alternative to punishment alone. Constantly directing their attention to *feelings, thinking* and *action* will teach children to do it for themselves. They will, in turn, ultimately develop the self-control they need in order to be successful in life. Discipline teaches them to reflect upon what should have happened and what alternative choices they can make when they feel like doing something against the rules. It requires them to go through the E-T-A sequence over and over until they are able to apply it *before,* rather than *after,* they act.

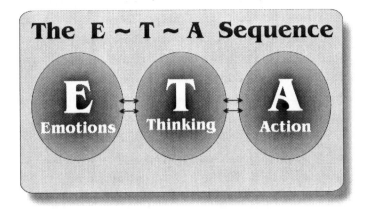

The 5 Simple Steps

The *5 Simple Steps* are simple communication and discipline strategies that help children develop the E-T-A sequence. They help develop thinking skills and self-control skills by reinforcing the appropriate brain sequence. This allows them to act properly even when they feel like acting improperly. I believe you will see positive change of even the most difficult behavior if you focus on these five simple strategies.

Please keep in mind that "simple" does not always mean "easy." Some of the strategies will require a genuine commitment to consistency. They will have to be practiced until they become natural for both the child and the adult. Maintaining consistency is not always easy. Sometimes the sequencing within our own brain gets out of order. That's when we act on our *feelings* instead of what we know to be the best course of *action*. An awareness of the *5 Simple Steps* will help you keep your own *feelings* from causing reactions that produce the wrong results in others. This will help you teach children to behave properly even when punishment has failed to do so.

The *5 Simple Steps* for discipline that works will help you understand why children can be punished for unacceptable behavior and still continue to do the same things that got them into trouble in the first place. They will also help you make the shift from an ineffective punishment mode to an effective discipline mode. Of course, the best way to teach respect for rules and self-control is to model behaviors we want from children.

If you consistently practice these strategies, you will experience the satisfaction of a teacher who once asked a first grader to think about the behavior that had caused him trouble. The teacher had placed the letters "E-T-A" on the wall so that the children could be reminded to think and reflect on their own behavior and think about the sequence that leads to good decisions. After an unhappy incident, the teacher asked a little boy to consider what had happened. The little boy stood studying the letters the teacher had placed on the wall. He momentarily had a look of puzzlement on his face. Finally, he looked at the teacher and said, "I think the 'A' got ahead of the 'T.'" The teacher, restraining the impulse to laugh, said, "Yes, I think that is exactly what happened. Now what are you going to do next time you have that *feeling*?" The discussion went on from there. She felt great satisfaction that this very impulsive little guy had made a giant step in the direction of self-control. He was becoming self-aware and was beginning to recognize that he did not think before he acted.

Teaching self-control to very impulsive, emotionally charged children has to happen in stages. Teaching self-awareness is the first stage. It is the beginning of good discipline and it does not always require punishment. It is not always an easy process. But if we do not teach this very important skill, most other attempts to discipline or punish will prove fruitless.

Teaching a child self-awareness and self-control is fundamental to success for a child in most areas of life. The teaching process may be challenging. The rewards, however, are many for both the adults who will teach and the children who will learn.

STEP **1** THINK FEELINGS

Adults are constantly challenged to help children and teens learn how to think clearly and wisely. Oftentimes, the greatest emphasis gets placed solely on the act of thinking. Feelings, however, are also a key component found in the process of good decision making. We frequently observe in children and teens how easily the emotional centers can override the thinking process. To understand child and adolescent behavior it is necessary to realize how this can happen so we can teach it to the children and teens in our care. The techniques discussed here can help them understand ways in which feelings can override thinking. This will improve their ability to think clearly and wisely. This chapter discusses some of the ways that young people can be taught to make good decisions through understanding the "feelings" part of the feeling-thinking-action process.

 Step 1 ~ Think Feelings

Feelings drive behavior. Most adults get so focused on getting children to think that they often overlook the point that it is emotions that most often precede behavior problems. For instance, two little boys start out with a simple rock-throwing contest. This is something little boys may find particularly enjoyable. At first, they are pretty aware of their surroundings and are careful about where they are throwing. The next thing you know, the competition heats up along with their excitement, and suddenly, somehow, a rock hits the neighbor's window...crash! Shortly thereafter, the boys are being questioned by angry parents and are claiming they don't know how the accident happened. Their parents are angry and frustrated because they are certain the boys knew better than to throw rocks at houses. These boys did know better. They just got caught up in the emotions of competition and triumph and somehow forgot what they knew. Their *feelings* overrode their *thinking* and ultimately dictated their behavior.

Every parent or teacher has many similar examples. Adults want to believe that once a child has been taught to do the right thing, the child will always remember and behave accordingly. Incidents of unacceptable behavior have left many an adult confounded because they are sure the child knew better. The adult concludes that the behavior was just willful disobedience and deserves punishment. This is often an erroneous assumption. The broken window was not a result of willful disobedience. It was a result of emotions that got a little carried away. The sequence, which should be *Emotions-Thinking-Action* — E-T-A — turned out to be *Emotions-Action-Thinking* — E-A-T.

Emotions are closely tied to needs. This is why emotions so often override *thinking*. There is the need to win, the need to be the best, or the need to prove you are the best. These needs are very powerful and can drive people to high-level success. Sometimes, however, it is one of these very same needs that can drive young people to accidentally break a window. The problem is neither the need itself nor the emotions that it can trigger. Rather, it is that most young people haven't yet learned the skills to move from *emotions* to *thinking*. This is especially true when the emotions are very intense. That is why it is so important for adults to *think feelings* when they are disciplining a child.

When we are able to consider a child's behavior in the context of the child's emotions, we can see more readily the necessity for keeping discipline focused on the connection between *emotions* and *thinking*. The child is taught to value the *thinking* process and to keep his *thinking* going even when he's excited. He is taught to be aware that when his focus is on the *feelings* of winning at all costs, he can lose track of where his entitlement to act ends and other people's property begins. Discussing this with a child should include a plan for what the child is going to do the next time he feels likes challenging a friend to a rock-throwing contest. A final step could be some sort of payment and certainly an apology for the broken window. In this example, discipline is about teaching the child to reflect on the events leading up to the accident, and not merely on what the boys should have been *thinking* before they threw the rocks. This may seem like a fine distinction, but consider how different the adult-child interaction is if the focus goes directly to the punishment mode.

If the child's window-breaking behavior in the above example is viewed as willful disobedience, then the lecture from the parents will be focused on "not thinking" and "being careless." Some parents might even feel that spanking is in order. In keeping with the punishment mode, the child has to suffer for his mistake. This may or may not teach him how to avoid the problem the next time. This approach is one reason parents find themselves saying, "If I've told you once, I've told you a thousand times!" Sound familiar? It becomes especially frustrating for adults, not to mention exhausting, when they begin to feel as if everything they say has to be repeated over and over again. Sometimes it even has the unfortunate effect of allowing a child to learn to *not* respond to a command. The result from this development is that the instructions have to be said repeatedly or at just a certain pitch in order for the child to "hear" them. Notice how skilled children and adolescents are at "tuning out." That is why it is so important for adults to stay in the teaching mode if they are determined to help a child change his behavior.

Be aware that there is a significant difference between *saying* something and *teaching* something. Teaching requires a discussion of the *process* of decision making, not just the outcome. It means talking about how something happened, not just *what* happened. It means focusing on something other than just the unsatisfactory result of faulty decision making. It requires the time and effort necessary to help the child focus on how both the *feeling* and *thinking* parts of the brain can work together.

One of the main goals of all discipline, parenting and educating is to help children arrive at a point in their adult lives where they are able to manage the process of self-control and good decision making on their own. The punishment mode, alone, has its limitations. It does not teach children self-control as much as it merely teaches them that adults can and will control their behavior for them. This is one of the reasons why the most severe punishment programs for chronic misbehavior, like the juvenile justice-style boot camps, have had great difficulty trying to consistently get the desired result.

The desired result of all punishment is to keep the young person from repeating the negative behavior. The boot camp programs have proven that they can get an out-of-control teenager under control. What they have failed to do is to teach the internal skills necessary to keep the child from re-offending or making the same unfortunate mistakes again and again. In the boot camp setting, it is the external authoritarian structure provided by the adults that results in compliant behavior. This, however, is not the same as teaching kids the internal skills to control themselves. Unfortunately, in most cases, when the juveniles are discharged, the skills and tools used for self-control stay behind within the hearts and minds of the boot camp adults.

When adults focus on the *emotions* that prompt unacceptable behavior, the child can begin to gain some understanding of his or her own behavior. Then children can be taught the skills they need in order to manage their reactions and responses to difficult situations. In the example of the stone throwing mentioned above, the parents may find themselves far more disturbed by the incident than the children themselves. They would probably ask the infamous question, *"What were you thinking?!"* Then the frustrating response comes forth: "I don't know." The scary thing is, the child is telling the truth. The incident had nothing to do with *thinking*. It had everything to do with *feeling*. That's why true discipline works best when adults *think feelings*.

Let's take an example of a child who keeps getting into trouble for the same thing over and over. A teenage girl seems angry all the time. She is often in verbal combat with her mother and several of her teachers. Each time she loses control and curses one of these adults, they respond with severe punishment. She loses privileges, including the use of the telephone and the car. This is a very severe consequence for most teenagers. In school, the girl is frequently sent to the office and given detention or suspension. This is often accompanied by a stern lecture about her disrespectful attitude. The girl is not belligerent. She always seems contrite...but there is always a next time.

The dialogue with her mother often sounds something like this:

Girl:	Mom, can I go over to Christy's house after school?
Mom:	No. You need to come home and get your chores done first.
Girl:	I won't be there long, and I'll do my chores as soon as I get home.

Mom:	That's what you said last time, and it didn't happen. The answer is no. I told you not to ask again!
Girl:	*(After many attempts to get her mother to relent, yelling)* You never let me do anything! All you care about is cleaning, cleaning, cleaning. You're such a #%*. I hate you!
Mom:	*(Also yelling)* That's it! You're grounded! No phone for a week. You better learn to watch your mouth!

In this example, the mother's only strategy is to fall back on punishment. Punishment is not achieving its goal because this is an oft-repeated scenario between the two of them. If the punishment had been effective, the girl would know that if she doesn't take "No" for an answer, and loses her temper, she will be punished. It has happened before. Sometimes punishment can even make the situation worse because teens can become "immune" to punishment. They adapt to living without privileges. They appear to become unconcerned about being sent to the office at school.

I have seen many middle and high school students who prefer in-school suspension because they find that they don't feel as angry or agitated in the highly structured environment of an in-school suspension room. It is less stressful than trying to deal with several irritating teachers or some scary fellow student throughout the day. Regardless of whether or not they prefer the so-called punishment, this approach does not allow them to learn the skills necessary for controlling their anger, impulses and behaviors that get them into trouble in the first place. This is similar to the girl in the above example who never learns the skills to control her temper. Her language never improves. The "punishment" no longer has its intended effect.

If the parents or teacher of this girl will *think feelings*, they can then focus on the *feelings* that are driving the behavior. This will help the girl find appropriate and acceptable ways to express her anger. More importantly, they can try to help her understand what *feelings* underlie the anger and what she needs to do to keep herself from losing control.[1] All this may take a little time, but with patience, persistence, and good modeling by the adults, she will learn how to get herself out of intense emotions and into healthy and effective *thinking*. A dialogue needs to take place.

When everyone is calm and in the *thinking* mode, it could go something like this:

Mom: I am concerned about you. You seem angry a lot of the time and I am hoping you and I can figure out what's bothering you. It seems to me there is something going on here that makes you feel agitated. Can you tell me what it is?

Girl: I don't know.

Mom: Try and guess. We need to figure out something so you don't have to lose your cool so often, and it will be a lot easier if we could figure out what you might be *feeling* that's making you angry. Could you be *feeling* hurt or resentful because you think I'm being unfair to you?

Girl: Yes. You always let Jan [the girl's older sister] do whatever she wants, but any time I ask to do something, you say no.

Mom: I regret that my decisions seem unfair.

---

[1] Note: Constant generalized anger in teenagers is often a symptom of clinical depression. If the anger persists over a period of weeks and either the parent or the adolescent seems confused at times about the origins of the anger, it is best to seek a medical evaluation or assessment for depression.

How about the next time you feel that way, you just calmly say, "This feels so unfair and it makes me mad!" Then we can talk about it without lots of screaming and nasty language. We may have to agree to disagree. You may not like my decision in the end, but it is important to be able to talk about what's bothering you. This needs to be done before you get to the point of *feeling* so much anger you can't *think* straight. Just say, "I'm SO mad!" I will listen. I need to tell you, though, that it is hard for me to listen to anything you are saying while you are yelling at me. Can we agree to try this?

Notice that the mother did not get defensive and say something such as, "Well, if you would do a few more things that I ask you to do, then I might be more inclined to let you do some of the things you want to do." She kept the focus on the issue of the way the girl was handling her emotions, not on the apparent cause of the anger. When an adult gets defensive or begins to lecture, the focus goes immediately back to the *content* of the argument and the age-old circular dance begins: *"I'm mad because you..." "Well, I'm mad because you..."*. Like most circles, it doesn't go anywhere. In the above example, the adult keeps the focus on the girl's tendency to lose control of her temper while at the same time attempting to teach her an alternative way to cope with her *feelings*. The parent also tries to help the girl figure out what she is really *feeling*. She doesn't get drawn into defending her decision to make the girl come home and do her chores.

Anger is always a secondary emotion[2]. It is usually an expression of some other *feeling*. *Feelings* usually come from some need or desire. In this example, it seems that the girl's anger is about not getting to do what she wants. When the mother asks the girl about her *feelings*, the girl perceives that her mother treats her sister differently. In this case, the *feeling* underlying the anger is most likely related to jealousy, envy, or even fear that her mother "loves her sister more." These are all common *feelings* that children and teens experience. If these *feelings* do not get acknowledged, they can develop into angry outbursts. Simply punishing children for inappropriate expression of anger will not help them figure all this out, nor will it help teach them to do the right thing when they get mad.

Perhaps all this girl needs is to be reassured that her mother's intention is to treat all her children equally even when it does not seem that way. Maybe the mother also needs to become aware of some possible unfairness in how she treats her children. Whatever the problem is, it is more than just the girl's terrible temper. The problem is that which is causing the anger. If adults will *think feelings*, they will begin to focus on underlying causes and will ultimately have a much better chance of getting the behavior changed. Whatever the *feelings* are, they will point to a need that has to be addressed. Once the *feelings* and needs get addressed, the behavior will change.[3]

In the school setting, children do have the ability to get sent to the office on multiple occasions. If someone took the time on each one of these occasions to discuss the child's *feelings* and *needs* with them, there would be a significant decrease in the number of students who get sent to the office for repeat offenses. Students with chronic behavior difficulties need help to figure out a better way to handle their emotions. One of the barriers against acting on this relatively simple process can be the fact that some adults are

---

[2] See *ABC's Workbook: Achieving Acceptable Behavior Changes*, Divinyi, 1999.

[3] See *Good Kids, Difficult Behavior*, Divinyi, 1998.

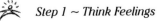

uncomfortable talking about *feelings*. Others are convinced that it would make no difference anyway or it would take too much time. It is strongly proposed here that it always does make a difference.

Here is an example of a situation experienced by teachers and administrators everywhere. The student has a history of behavior problems during Fifth Period every day. He is frequently sent to the office for disrupting the class. He's even been suspended in the past for his disruptive behavior. His parents are supportive of the school and have also punished him for getting into trouble. He still shows up in the office at least once a week. This is a dialogue between the boy and an Assistant Principal who took the time to consider what might be causing the disruptive behavior:

AP:	Well, here we are at Fifth Period again and you have come to visit me again. Tell me, son, what's your problem with Fifth Period?
Student:	Nothing.
AP:	Are you saying you like your Fifth Period class?
Student:	No.
AP:	What class is it?
Student:	Social Studies.
AP:	So you don't like Social Studies?
Student:	No. It's boring.
AP:	You would not be the first person to think so. What happens when you get bored?
Student:	I don't know.
AP:	Well it looks like you find a way to make the class interesting by getting into some struggle with the teacher. Isn't that the way it looks to you?
Student:	Yes sir.

AP:	What do you say you and I try to figure out something for you to do when you are bored other than hassling the teacher and disrupting the class? You don't have to like Social Studies, but you do have to pass the class. Since you are a pretty smart guy, I think we can figure this out. You don't need to be down here every time I turn around. Okay?
Student:	Okay.
AP:	Sometimes when I'm bored in a class, I like to draw while I'm taking notes. My guess is you can draw and listen at the same time. What do you think? If you were drawing something, something appropriate now, while the teacher was talking, maybe you could keep from being overcome with boredom and getting yourself in trouble. What do you say?
Student:	I don't think the teacher is going to like it. I tried it once and she took my paper and threw it away.
AP:	What if I talk to her and she agrees that you can draw or doodle as long as you do not interrupt the class. How's that sound? Do you think you could manage that? We all have to have "boredom skills" because there are just going to be a lot of things that bore you in life that still need to be done. If drawing or doodling doesn't work as a good

	"boredom skill" for you, or the teacher doesn't like my idea, then you ask to see me and we'll try to think of something else. In the meantime, can you keep yourself out of trouble in Fifth Period?
Student:	Yes sir.
AP:	Okay, come see me after school tomorrow and let me know how it's going.

Note that the administrator kept the focus on the *feelings* that were driving the chronic misbehavior. He did not dwell yet again on the details of what happened. His goal was to get the behavior changed, not prove that he had the power and authority to punish. Many teachers have discovered that making thoughtful accommodations, which help meet a child's specific need, will lead to significant behavior improvement.

Do not misunderstand. Punishment is sometimes necessary. Children or teens should be held accountable for their mistakes. Consequences may be in order. It may be perfectly appropriate to punish a child or adolescent for being disrespectful, especially for cursing at her mother or a teacher. However, we have to remember that the punishment itself will not teach the student how to handle his emotions. Punishment will not teach him how to get from the *E* part of the brain to the *T* part of the brain. Regardless of how often he is made to suffer for his mistakes, he still has to *learn* this *E* to *T* skill or he will continually repeat the same behavior.

It may be a requirement of the School-Wide Discipline Plan that the student be sent, yet again, to in-school suspension. Unless someone takes the time to help him figure out what *feelings* are driving the chronic misbehavior, this pattern will continue. The practice of *thinking* and focusing on the *feelings* that prompt unacceptable behavior, and discussing the *feelings* with the child, can add a new and powerful dimension to any effort to teach a child self-control and respect for rules.

Keep in mind that the first attempt to have such a conversation might not go as smoothly as the examples given above, but if you give it a try you will probably find that it certainly won't make anything worse. The point is to move from the obvious problem (disrupting the class) or content of the argument (wanting to go somewhere without doing chores) to the *feelings* behind them. In the example of the girl and her mother, the obvious problem was a hot temper and disrespectful behavior. This behavior only appeared to arise from the girl not getting to do something she wanted to do. She really had other things going on as well.

The goal is to move the discussion from the unacceptable behavior to the sequence of emotions or events that stimulate intensely angry *feelings* which drive the behavior. Once the girl is focused on how she is managing her emotions, what she is really *feeling,* and how that makes her *act,* then the parents or teachers can help her find a healthier way to handle those *feelings.* They can help her figure out what she needs for those *feelings* to change. Once she can keep her emotions from taking control, she will have a much better chance of changing the behavior that keeps getting her into trouble.

Watch parents or teachers who seem to have well disciplined children. Watch how they interact with their children. They don't seem concerned about making the point that they are the boss, the one in charge or the one in control. Instead, they seem to be constantly teaching. The best disciplinarians are the most confident that it is their job to teach children *how* to behave. They don't seem to have to punish their children very often. Every incident of negative behavior becomes an opportunity to teach the child something new.

I always notice how parents interact with their children in public. For instance, children are notoriously unconscious of other

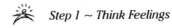

people's space. Consequently, it is not uncommon to see a parent scolding a child for bumping into someone because they weren't paying attention. One parent might simply take the child by the hand and, eye to eye, explain why it is not okay to run into other people. Another may take a very different approach.

After a bumping incident:

Parent A:	Watch what you are doing! Can't you see you are bumping into people? You never pay attention to what you are doing. I get tired of having to tell you the same thing all the time. The next time I have to tell you, we won't be stopping at Baskin Robbins before we leave the mall. Now pay attention!

Versus

Parent B:	Watch out now! What do you need to say to the lady?
Child:	Excuse me.
Parent:	What else?
Child:	I'm sorry.
Parent:	Good. Now what do you need to do?
Child:	Pay attention.
Parent:	Thank you very much. I knew you could do it. Now let's go and be sure to watch for other people.

Consider the difference between punishing a child for this very common error and disciplining the child. Both parents mean well. Both want to teach the child to pay attention to the people around them. Which do you think is most likely to be successful?

Think feelings. How do you think the child of parent A was *feeling* after he was scolded? How do you think the child of Parent B felt? Which child do you think is most likely to stay alert? Parents often unwittingly cause their children to feel stupid or inept. Feeling stupid can cause us to act stupidly. We all tend to do most things better when we don't feel stupid. It's always better to help children feel smart and able. The manner in which we point out mistakes can make a big difference as to whether or not the criticism will have the desired results. If you are attuned to the child's *feelings* when you are teaching him or her to behave properly, you are much more likely to get good results.

Which child in the above example do you think is most likely to want to obey? Don't you feel more inclined to follow the directions of someone who thinks well of you and also makes the assumption that you have good intentions and are capable? Most of us do. Children are particularly sensitive to getting their *feelings* hurt. Once they are hurt, the child is far less likely to want to obey.

I expect that some readers are saying right now, "I don't care so much how he *feels* or if he likes it! I do care if he does what I tell him! It never occurred to my parents to worry about my feelings. I just knew I had better do what I was told!" This may be true for a lot of us. It does not, however, necessarily make for the best, or the most effective, or even the only way to discipline children. At this time in history, we do many things differently from what our parents did, even though we love and respect what our parents tried to do for us. The world is a very different place than it was when many of us were growing up. Sometimes a style of parenting that is different from our own childhood experience can be very helpful. Parents and teachers are often determined to follow the rules of discipline and punishment that worked with them when they were children. This is all fine and good if the strategies are getting the desired results. Is the child following direction, learning self-control and developing a healthy sense of self-esteem? Is the child emotionally healthy? I have seen very abusive parents easily keep a child under control. I have seen children readily obey because they were literally afraid for their lives. Though these parents can appear to

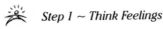

maintain control over their children, they almost certainly damage their children's emotional health. This negative, non-teaching approach causes all manner of unhealthy, or even anti-social, behavior.

Getting the best results from discipline requires adults to think about two different aspects of the child's feelings. The first is to think about what feelings are driving the child's behavior. The second is to consider how the child feels after the discipline has happened. It is okay for a child to feel unhappy after being disciplined. They cannot be expected to be happy when they are being punished. Their "unhappiness," however, should not arise from being made to feel humiliated, stupid or scared. Intense negative feelings will only prompt more negative behavior. It is important to have an acute awareness of the child's feelings at the time the discipline is being applied. It is not useful to teach children obedience if their self-confidence is destroyed in the process. Self-confidence is one of the fundamentals of self-discipline. For us to control our behavior, we have to have a certain amount of confidence in our own ability to do the right thing. Children who are made to feel stupid each time they make a mistake will have a difficult time learning to have confidence in themselves. It isn't necessary to make children or teenagers feel bad about themselves in order to help them learn from their mistakes and develop self-control.

Notice the differences in the following examples:

Parent A:	I noticed your room didn't get cleaned as I asked.
Teen:	I'm going to do it.
Parent A:	And when might that be?
Teen:	After this program is over.
Parent A:	Do it now, please.
Teen:	This is almost over.
Parent A:	Now. Please! (*Turns off TV.*)

It is not necessary to have discussions about *feelings* each and every time. It *is* necessary, each and every time, to avoid attacking or diminishing the personhood or the character of the child. Most people, and children are no exception, have intense negative feelings about anyone who is attacking them. Children, especially teenagers, are far more likely to cooperate and obey people if they believed they are liked.

Consider this example:

Parent B:	You didn't clean your room again! I'm sick of telling you about it!
Teen:	I'm going to get to it!
Parent B:	I'm tired of hearing that too! Just because you don't mind living like a slob doesn't mean the rest of us are willing to live that way!
Teen:	I said I'd do it!
Parent B:	Go do it right now or you can forget that date you're planning tonight! I don't know what boy would want to go out with anybody whose room looks like a pigsty!
Teen:	He doesn't go in my room!
Parent B:	That's not the point! The point is you are lazy and irresponsible and no decent boy is going to want somebody who can't even pick up her underwear off the floor!

In the first example, the issue stayed focused on the point of getting the room cleaned in the time frame the parent demanded. The teen probably was not happy about having to clean or getting the TV turned off. He or she was probably good and mad. Feeling angry, in this case, is understandable and even okay. However, it is

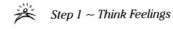

a different kind of anger from that of the teen in the second example. In the second scenario, the issue became the teen's character and not her dirty room. Not only does the parent insult her character, but she also questions how anyone else could like the teen. This kind of insult can leave a teenager hurt and angry and much less inclined to do what the parent wants.

Many parents seem to think that, since it is their job to shape the character of their children, they are entitled to make negative comments, even insulting comments, that they wouldn't dare say to someone else. But an insult is an insult. It makes people feel bad. It makes them feel angry. What is the point of making people angry when you want them to do something? The angry feelings just get in the way.

This type of exchange happens in school every day, even with well meaning teachers:

Teacher: Where is your paper?

Student: I don't know. I can't find it.

Teacher: We've talked before about your lack of organization and responsibility. It is your responsibility to get your assignments in on time. If you aren't going to be responsible and stay organized enough to get them in, don't expect me to feel sorry for you when your parents want to know why your grades went down. It's certainly not my fault!

The teacher means well. Many teachers believe that it is their responsibility to help their students develop character. This is even a legislated expectation in more and more school systems across the country. This can tempt some of us in the teaching profession to make a "character" issue out of too many things that children do. He lost his assignment — that makes him "irresponsible." Some even believe that the best way to teach "responsibility" is to continually point out when it is "lacking." Being constantly reminded of one's shortcomings usually makes people angry or disheartened. This is discouraging. Adults need to use encouragement with children, especially when teaching them to work out their shortcomings.

Consider another scenario:

Teacher:	Where is your paper?
Student:	I don't know. I can't find it.
Teacher:	I'm sorry about that. It is due today. What do you think you need to do to find and get it in to me tomorrow?
Student:	I guess I can look for it.
Teacher:	Maybe you could get someone to help you look for it.
Student:	My Mom will help me look.
Teacher:	Good. Then maybe you could ask her to help you be sure to get it here tomorrow. You are smart and capable and I want you to be able to get the grades you deserve. To be fair to the other students, I'll have to take points off for being late. The important thing to me is that you did it. If you get help learning to be more organized so you can get things in on time, you'll be able to prove to your parents that you're just as smart as I know you are.

In the second example, the teacher did not cut the child any slack for not having the paper, nor did she make the problem a character issue. In fact, she set about affirming the child's intelligence. She also made suggestions about the need for more organization and the prospect of getting help from someone else. After all, isn't this what most "organizationally impaired" adults do? We should expect that the student in the second example walked away feeling good, and more determined to find his assignment and get it to the teacher. The student in the first example probably had a different response.

In both examples, the student suffered the consequences for losing his paper, but in the second example the teacher let the consequences work for themselves. He didn't feel obliged to give the consequence of a lecture, right on top of the first consequence. Instead he showed compassion and confidence in the student.

Compassion and confidence are highly effective tools for discipline. When children experience compassion and know that adults have confidence in them to do the right thing, they learn to develop those beliefs about themselves and others. What does our world need more of than a constant renewal of compassionate and courageous people? All people need to have their *feelings* acknowledged. To acknowledge feelings is not to concede that we agree with them. It is simply to say, "Yes, I understand what you're feeling or experiencing." In the above example, the teacher tells the boy that he is sorry that the boy is not going to get his assignment in on time. He's saying "I feel bad for you" instead of berating the boy. This strategy gets much better results. Don't we wish someone at the bank would say something like that when we call to tell them we accidentally forgot to mail our check on time? Whether we pay a late fee or not, we will probably be more careful and responsive to people who treat us with respect and compassion whether we actually deserve it or not.

The ability to tune into another person's emotions is a learned skill, and it begins with an awareness of our own emotions. Children who develop what Daniel Goleman calls *emotional intelligence* do so by being taught about feelings.[4] They become aware at a very early age that *feelings* are important. This includes the *feelings* of others. They learn that feelings do not have to control a person or

---

[4] See *Emotional Intelligence*, Goleman, 1995.

control the situation in which they find themselves. They do learn that feelings are very important indicators of what is really going on. Notice the next time you walk into a situation that just doesn't feel right. You find yourself thinking, "What's really going on here?" You will be inclined to trust your *feeling senses* because the *feeling sense* is a "first alert system" in our brains. According to Gavin de Becker, author of *Gift of Fear*, the feeling sense that we call intuition is very reliable in sensing danger. People can get hurt if they always let their *thinking* process override their fearful *feelings*. This can lead to the erroneous conclusion that there is no danger.

I use these examples to emphasize the importance of the emotional realm of our brain. All brains are composed of the same basic hardware. There are parts for *thinking* and parts for *feeling*. In our culture, we tend to ignore the importance of the *feeling* part of the brain because we aren't comfortable with the language of *feelings*.

It is reasonably easy to acknowledge a child's feelings. We learn that it helps enormously to move them from the *emotion* mode to the *thinking* mode. It is almost as though a child's *feelings* cannot diminish without being acknowledged first. Before we can change the behavior by teaching the E-T-A process, *thinking* gets second place in line. This process of acknowledging a child's or teenager's *feelings* isn't difficult. It can, however, feel awkward if you aren't used to it. Let me give a couple of examples of emotional acknowledgement. In each of these scenarios, the child is struggling over getting her homework accomplished.

Child: I hate this! It's stupid! My teacher thinks that none of us has a life and that all we should do is work, work, work!

(The child gets up to leave without finishing her homework.)

Parent:	Whoa! Come on back. I hate it for you, and I admit it does seem like a lot of homework for one night but if you just keep at it, you'll get it done a lot sooner.

Versus

Child:	I hate this! It's stupid! My teacher thinks that no one has a life and that all we should do is work, work, work.

(The child gets up to leave without finishing her homework.)

Parent:	Quit fussing and just get it done! It is NOT stupid and you better remember that when you have to take the test!

Or

Child:	I got an 89 on my math test. One crummy point and I could have had an A. You'd think the teacher would cut a little slack once in awhile!
Parent:	What a bummer. I know you're disappointed. You worked hard.

Versus

Parent:	What did you get on the math test?
Child:	89.
Parent:	89! See, I told you to study harder, but NO ... you had to play video games! Those games aren't going to help you at report card time!

Which child is more likely to work a little harder the next time? The first parent simply acknowledged the child's disappointment, and then put the emphasis on what the child had done right. The second emphasized the negative, and coupled it with a negative prediction. Sometimes parents and teachers are prone to negative predictions. They think this will serve as a warning to the child, but find out that it usually does the exact opposite. Predictions, as we know, can have a nasty way of transforming themselves into expectations. They say to the child, "I expect you to screw up." We have all learned that children have a way of living up, or down, to our expectations.

Even when a child and an adult are arguing, it can be effective to acknowledge the child's feelings regardless of whether you agree with their point.

Adult:	I said no.
Child:	But you said I could go if I did...
Adult:	That is not what I said.
Child:	But all my friends are going.
Adult:	Look, I know this is frustrating for you, and I hate it for you, but the answer is still no. I'm sorry.

Versus

Adult:	I said no! Don't ask again.
Child:	But you said I could go if I did what you said.
Adult:	You just love to twist what I said! I did not say that you could go. You didn't do what you were told to do, and you have no one to blame but yourself! Too bad! Get over it!

It is hard to stay focused on effective communication in the heat of a verbal conflict. We discover, though, that the more we practice *thinking* about *feelings*, the more natural it becomes. Emotions punctuate our lives. They can mark the beginning and the ending of a sequence of events. Paying attention to the feelings after the fact can make as much difference as paying attention to the feelings that are driving the behavior in the first place. Whether before or after, it will significantly increase your success in teaching children self-control and helping them develop self-confidence if you *think feelings.*

Summary

The brain is organized in a way that allows different areas to accomplish different tasks. One part of the brain makes it possible to *feel* and another part makes it possible to *think*. It is the interaction of these two parts of the brain that causes people to act the way they do. Children and teens are much more likely to act on what they are *feeling* than on what they are *thinking*.

Sometimes they act without *thinking* at all. Their intense *feelings* can override the good judgment that resides in the *thinking* part of the brain. When children keep making the same mistake over and over, even after they have been punished repeatedly, then it is necessary for adults to figure out what *feelings* are driving their behavior. Then adults have to teach them how to *think* about a different and acceptable way to manage those *feelings.*

The entire purpose of discipline is to teach children how to manage their own behavior and help them develop self-control. There is, however, a significant difference between discipline and punishment. To discipline is to teach, or it is not discipline. Punishment may make a child sorry for a mistake, but it won't necessarily *teach* the child how to handle a situation differently the next time it happens. Adults need to stay focused on teaching children *how* to do the right thing. Even when punishment is necessary and appropriate, it isn't helpful or necessary to make kids feel humiliated or stupid because they made a mistake.

Children and teens have strong *feelings* about the way adults interact with them. It is always best to pay attention to the *feelings* of the children and teens in your care because they are much more likely to make good decisions and choices when their *feelings* are not agitated or angry. Adults do not need to hurt kids' *feelings* when they are disciplining them. It is usually counterproductive to do so. When children feel hurt and angry, they are less likely to obey or to exercise self-control.

Staying aware of a child or teen's *feelings* will help most discipline strategies work more effectively. Compassion and acknowledgement of their *feelings* will help teach children to pay attention to their own emotions. It will also help them begin to recognize the difference between *feeling* and *thinking*. They will learn how each is important and necessary to the process of making good decisions. They will also learn to become aware of other people's *feelings*, which will ultimately give them the greatest potential for success in life.

.

STEP 2 ASK QUESTIONS

The second principle for making discipline work is to ask questions. There are two aspects of asking questions that foster positive behavior change. The first is to use questions to teach self-awareness and redirect behavior. The second is to ask questions for the purpose of assessment. This means asking questions to discover the emotions and thinking patterns that prompt chronic negative behavior patterns. These two aspects of using questions as an effective discipline tool will be discussed in this chapter.

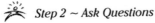

Ask Questions To Teach Self-awareness

Teaching children how to manage or control their own behavior is not as easy as we sometimes wish it were. One reason it becomes difficult to teach these skills is that we sometimes tend to forget that children are rarely paying close attention in the first place. We all know it is hard to learn anything at all if one is not paying attention to what is being taught. What we don't always realize is that the child may not be "paying attention" even to himself! Kids are capable of being utterly clueless about what's going on around them, or they can seem to be unconscious about what they might be doing at any given moment.

The first step toward getting children to make good choices is to get them to pay attention to what they are doing. There are two ways to do this. One is to constantly point out to them what they are doing and then command them to do something else. This can work and is sometimes the best bet. When a child is in danger, it is important that he or she has already been taught to respond to a command. Many a child has been saved from disaster by obeying the simple command, "Stop!" It is a good thing to teach children to respond to verbal commands. Teaching children to respond to a voice command starts when children are very young. It requires parents to get up and go after the child who is ignoring them after the first time the child fails to respond to verbal directions by an adult. The child needs to be moved to do what he is told to do. Children don't necessarily need to be punished, but they do need to know that they are not going to be told twice, or even begged to respond, before the parent takes action. It concerns me that so many parents do not seem to be able to do this.

Another way to teach children to pay attention and respond to adult directions is to frequently ask them questions. Questions require a response, which in turn triggers the *thinking* process.

Asking questions instead of making commands works like this:

The child is running through the house.

Mother: Hey, what are you supposed to do in the house?

Girl: Walk.

Mother: Can you do that please?

Versus

Mother: Hey, quit running, right now.

The first example seems to take longer, but it has the added benefit of calling attention to what the child is supposed to do. At the same time it lets the child acknowledge what she is doing wrong. This process builds self-awareness and teaches responsibility. The second example may seem more practical because it is most direct, but it puts more responsibility for the child's behavior on the mother than on the child. Even though the child may stop running in both versions, the second version does not require the child to pay attention or to think about what she's doing, or more importantly, what she should be doing.

It is also true that when children are trained only to pay attention to a parent or some other external authority, they can sometimes have trouble learning to develop an internal awareness of what they are doing when unsupervised. It is certainly important to teach children to respond to external authority. It can be lifesaving. It is also very important to teach them skills to develop internal authority, by becoming self-aware. They need to learn to pay attention to what they are doing and to make their own internal decisions about an appropriate response and what would be the best *action* to take without being told by an adult. Self-awareness is the beginning of developing internal authority.

When little children come into my office, they sometimes have to be reminded to take their feet off the couch. Their parents are trying to teach them to be respectful of other people's property as well as proper behavior outside their home.

Some parents give a simple command: "Put your feet down!"

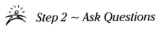

Others give commands and add on a few more lessons. They say things such as: "You know better than that. You're not at home. I've told you to keep your feet off other people's furniture."

But some parents will simply look at the child and ask: "Excuse me. Where are your feet?"

In all these situations, the children usually respond to their parents. In the last example, though, the parent not only directed the child to get his feet off the furniture, but she helped teach her child self-awareness. She taught her child to pay attention to his own body, not just pay attention to her. Children need help learning to pay attention to what they are doing. The best way to do this is to use questions when making commands or giving directions.

When you ask a question, it puts the child in the position of having to think as well as respond. When the answer to the question requires them to state something about themselves, then they begin to pay attention to their own behavior. This, in turn, teaches them self-control.

Using questions to teach self-awareness, and ultimately personal responsibility, has four basic steps.

Step 1: *Clarify the positive behavior standards expected.*
Step 2: *Ask questions that call attention to behavior.*
Step 3: *Wait for an answer.*
Step 4: *Redirect to proper behavior.*

Step 1: Clarify Positive Behavior Standards

Keep The Rules Positive

First, make sure that the standards of acceptable behavior are very clear. Many times adults believe that if children know the rules and know what they are supposed to do or not do, they will do the right thing. Unfortunately it takes more than knowing. Knowledge of the rules is not necessarily enough. Good behavior takes practice, and practice sometimes means going over and over the rules. It is a fundamental part of the training process that the young have to repeat lessons, even if it seems as though they had already been learned. How those repetitions are done can be very important. I will discuss this further in Chapter 5.

When reminding children of the rules, keep the focus on positive behavior. As often as possible, state rules or commands in terms of what you want the child *to do*, rather than what *not to do*. A positive goal-oriented focus is far more effective than continually stating what you *do not* want. It helps remind and teach the child what he needs to do.

This may mean that some of the common rules or commands have to be re-stated in a positive format.

For instance, if you have the rule that children don't argue with their parents, consider stating your expectations in a positive manner. Consider the following examples.

Negative command:

Adult: Don't talk back!"
         (Usually repeated over and over)

It is better to say:

Adult: Take no for an answer.

or

Do it now.

or

Please do as I said now.

One command tells the child what not to do. The others tell the child what to do or call the child's attention to the original command. All three address the same issue, but one points the child in the direction you want her to go. The other just tells her what not to do. Be clear in your directions and commands to children and teens. Let them know exactly what you want them to do even if you are angry or upset. When the mission is to teach children to behave, it is best to keep the focus on positive behavior.

Even the most well meaning parents and teachers sometimes forget to keep the focus on positive expectations. Rules are necessary, but many times the rules point to the things you *do not* want instead of what you *do* want. For instance, the rule "Don't talk while the teacher's talking" can easily be restated as "One person talks at a time." This keeps the focus on what the child is supposed to do. It also reinforces the courtesy necessary to conduct a class.

Some examples of positively versus negatively focused rules are:

↑ Be kind to others.

Versus

↓ Don't ridicule or make fun of others.

↑ Keep your hands to yourself.

Versus

↓ Don't touch.

↑ Talk respectfully to others.

Versus

↓ Don't talk back to adults.

↑ Be on time.

Versus

↓ Don't be late.

↑ Do it the first time.

Versus

⬇ Don't make me tell you twice.

⬆ Walk in the hall.

Versus

⬇ Don't run in the hall.

Ownership In The Rules Helps Children Respond

Clarifying behavior standards can be even more effective when children and teens have ownership in the development of the rules. I like doing this whenever possible because it gives the children some ownership in keeping things running well. I usually ask kids that I'm working with if they can agree to a few guidelines which will make things run smoothly for everyone. Depending on the setting, whether it is a large group, a class, or a private office, I discuss what I am going to do and what I will need for them to do in order for us to accomplish our task. Then I ask them if we can agree with these simple rules or standards. They are usually ready to agree, simply because they are not accustomed to an adult *asking* them to behave properly and respectfully.

Once they have agreed, they have taken responsibility for their *action*s. Now, if things don't go well, I can ask them about the agreements they made or what exactly they are doing.

When a child continues to interrupt I might say:

Me: Excuse me. What was our agreement?
Child/teen: One person talks at a time.
Me: Thank you. You will get your turn to talk.

In a family setting, there isn't a need to get agreements for all the rules and regulations. After all, it is the parent's responsibility to make the rules and see to it that children follow them. Still, asking questions is another way to remind children of the rules and their

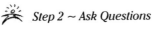 *Step 2 ~ Ask Questions*

responsibility to follow them. It is also healthy for parents to discuss the "why" of rules. This doesn't mean that parents should have to get permission from a child to make a rule. Getting kids to follow the rules works better when they are allowed to participate in the process. Participation will help them better understand why the rules exist in the first place. Having some responsibility in rule making will also help children learn how everyone has to live by rules and agreements in order for families to get along well and take care of each other.

Detailed Directions Help

Rules give us structure and order. Children and adolescents need plenty of structure. Structure simply means clearly defined directions, limits and boundaries. The more difficult a child's behavior is, the more detailed the directions need to be and the more positively they need to be stated.

When I was working with a group of ADHD (Attention Deficit Hyperactive Disorder) boys from the ages of 5 to 12, I found very quickly that they needed much more detailed direction than children who did not have to deal with the challenge of ADHD.

For instance, if I would normally say: "Everyone sit down and listen up," I would need to be much more directive with them: "Put your bottom in the chair. Put both feet on the floor. Keep all four chair legs on the floor. Keep your eyes on me. Only one person talks at a time."

That kind of detailed direction is not always necessary, but it helps enormously with children who aren't always conscious of what they are doing. It also keeps the focus on what they *need to do*, instead of what you *do not want* them to do.

By using detailed direction, I avoided having to constantly say, "Don't lean back in the chair. Keep your hands to yourself. Look at me when I'm speaking and quit talking while I'm talking." The first scenario is more pro-active, and I soon found out it did not take as much energy as the second.

Step 2: Use Questions To Call Attention To Behavior

Kids Can Be Clueless

I can hear some reader saying, "Oh, my son/student knows the rules, he just doesn't care." There may be some truth in that statement, but knowing the rules is one thing, and being conscious of them, and being aware of what one is doing at all times, is another matter. Children have to be taught to pay attention to what they are doing at a given moment. The best way to teach self-awareness is to constantly call their attention to what they are doing. This method does not require nagging or constant chastising. It does require questions.

The most frequently asked question should be: "Excuse me, what are you doing?"

You will be amazed how often the child or teen in question has to literally do a momentary check-in to see what they are doing. They need that check-in. They can be, and often are, totally oblivious of what they are doing. I've seen children crawl under a chair or table and not even realize they have done it.

Children and teens need to be coached to pay attention to what they are doing. Often parents or teachers will assume that a child who appears oblivious just does not care. It is much more likely that they are simply not aware. The "What are you doing?" question is a coaching tool. It doesn't need to be said like an accusation or be delivered with sarcasm. A tone of voice that implies that the child is stupid or clueless will only make them defensive. A negative or hostile tone of voice will put the focus on you and not on them. It will not call their attention to their own behavior.

Occasionally, I will address a teenager whose body language is very threatening and ask them to freeze long enough to look at what their body is doing. Many times they have no clue that they are "up in someone's face" and will usually readily back off once they are aware. They have not yet learned to self-observe. Without some

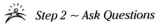

idea of what they are doing at a given moment, it is hard for them to change their behavior. This is even truer of little children.

For instance, when a child is running when they are supposed to walk, it is sometimes necessary to just say, "Walk!" Other times, it is helpful to point out what they are doing and let them make the correction. Asking, "What are you doing?" can be the simple reminder they need, because it requires them to check in with themselves, not just obey.

Questions Teach Responsibility

Another benefit of using questions to teach self-awareness and redirect behavior is that it allows children the opportunity to take responsibility for their *actions*. The word "responsibility" is a favorite of parents and educators. It means simply the ability to respond, or response-ability. It is an important character trait to foster in children, but it can't be taught unless children are made aware of what they are doing and what they need to be doing. Acknowledgement of an *action* is the first step in taking responsibility. Teaching responsibility works best by letting the child do just that.

Adults can inadvertently take the responsibility for the child's action by saying:

"I told you not to do that. I could scream when you don't listen to me. You *will* listen to me. I will not tolerate you thinking you can ignore me."

Without meaning to, this adult is telling the child that she, the adult, is not really in control, but that she believes she will make the child do the right thing. The reality is that you cannot *make* a child behave. The above example illustrates that the issues of control in this interchange belong to the adult. The focus needs to be redirected to the child's ability to control his own behavior. The questioning method puts the focus where it needs to be.

It works best to teach personal responsibility by asking questions and keeping the focus on the child's behavior, not on your authority.

Adult:	What are you doing?
Child:	Watching TV.
Adult:	What did I say?
Child:	Turn it off.
Adult:	Then what do you need to do now?
Child:	Turn it off.
Adult:	Now, please!

Now the emphasis is focused on the child's behavior and the child's responsibility to do what needs to be done.

When adults get too caught up in their own authority and proving that they have all the power, they can inadvertently end up taking the responsibility for the child's behavior instead of teaching the child to take responsibility for himself. When this happens children will have a tendency to forget what they are doing, or what they are supposed to do, until the adult calls them to task. These children do pretty much what they want until they get caught doing something unacceptable. They do not learn to take ownership of their own behavior.

Step 3: **Wait For An Answer**

Don't forget to let children answer your question. Not only do they need to be made aware of what they are doing, they need to take ownership of their behavior. That's why you need to wait for them to respond to your question. Your question is not meant to be rhetorical. It needs an answer, and the answer requires them to acknowledge what they are doing.

For example, if a teacher (T) stops a student (S) from running in the hall, she would say:

T/Question:	Excuse me, what are you doing?

Wait for an answer:

S/Answer:	Running in the hall.

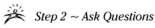

Here is another example of waiting for an answer when a child is questioned about inappropriate behavior:

T/Question:	Excuse me, freeze for a moment. Where is your hand?
	Wait for an answer:
S/Answer:	In her face.
T/Question:	Where should it be?
	Wait for an answer:
S/Answer:	At my side.
T/Question:	Can you put it there please?
	Wait for an answer:
S/Answer:	Yes sir.

The answer requires them to use the *thinking* part of their brain for just a minute.

They need to think about what they are doing. Unless the child has a chance to answer your question, you might as well just tell them to stop, or give some other command. Their personal on-the-spot answer gives them the opportunity to remember what they *should* be doing. It also reminds them that their behavior is in their own control. Since discipline is meant to teach self-control, this strategy continuously asks them to control their own behavior (internally) rather than relying on you to control it (externally).

Step 4: Redirect To Proper Behavior

Calling attention to a young person's behavior, asking a question and waiting for an answer gives you the opportunity to redirect inappropriate behavior. More importantly, it gives them the opportunity to correct their own behavior. It also allows you to address a behavior without necessarily having to punish the child for breaking a rule.

After you have waited for an answer and the child responds, then ask them if they can do what they are supposed to do. The best follow-up questions for teaching them to pay attention and follow directions are:

Adult:	What are you supposed to be doing?

Wait for an answer...

Child:	Walking in the halls.
Adult:	Could you do it now?

After the child complies...

Adult:	Thank you very much.

Again, asking them to state what they are supposed to be doing is more effective than commanding them to do something. For some children a question will work when a command will not. Children who tend to be oppositional by nature will often respond properly to a request, but can become automatically defiant in response to a command. In fact, the above "request" is a "command." It is simply a different way of stating a command. You are not giving them the option to continue doing what they want to do. However, in most instances, it is unnecessary to apply force or a threat. When you use questions and answers you make it very clear that your expectation is that they *will* do what you want them to do. Your expectations are powerful. Usually, children will live up to the expectations we set forth. It is important to make positive expectations a routine part of daily interactions.

Notice the difference when the follow-up questions express a negative expectation:

Adult:	What should you be doing?

Not waiting for an answer...

Adult:	Why don't you ever do what you are told? I have to tell you all the time because you never listen.

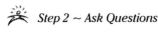

The above statements may be accurate in that the adult does have to tell the child over and over. However, it still does not put the focus on acceptable behavior. Instead, it places the focus on the unacceptable behavior. Things that receive focused attention seem to expand. Teachers who constantly remind their students that they never listen quite frequently find that they have students who never listen.

Some adults find it difficult to stay focused on positive expectations. It is not uncommon for parents who love their children dearly to be unable to praise them or affirm their belief that they will make good behavior choices. Yet there are many young teens who make good but difficult decisions and who still manage to avoid the inappropriate or illegal behaviors of their peers. They often do so because they want to live up to the positive expectations their parents have communicated to them. They know their parents expect them to do the right thing. They do not want to experience their parents' disappointment. This isn't quite the same as being afraid of getting caught, or getting into trouble. It is more powerful. When the only reason not to do something wrong stems from the fear of getting caught, it can become easier to decide to risk it and take your chances. When the reason for maintaining good behavior is a need to live up to your parents' faith in you and their positive expectations, it is harder to step over the line.

Now that the steps for using questions to teach self-awareness and give directions and commands have been identified, it is helpful to review once again the difference between punishment and discipline.

Don't Let Punishment
Get In The Way Of Discipline

When children and teens do step over the line, or refuse to respond to commands, punishment may seem necessary. Punishment, however, isn't always the powerful behavior management tool adults would like for it to be. It can even get in the way of effective discipline. Effective discipline only requires getting children redirected to what they need to be doing and then teaching them how to do it. Asking questions to teach self-awareness and redirecting behavior is especially important when punishment fails to obtain the desired results.

The punishment mode requires that mistakes and rule breaking *have* to be punished. Sometimes they do. The whole point of punishment, though, is to get behavior changed. Often this does not happen. One reason for this is that administering punishment can get so time consuming. It can require so many time-consuming activities, such as timeout discussions, taking privileges away, trips back and forth to the school office — that adults will often choose to overlook mistakes and broken rules just to avoid having to repeatedly punish a child. This adult reluctance to follow through with consequences encourages children, who can be natural born gamblers, to continue negative behavior. They tend to think that maybe this time they will get away with it.

Another reason that punishment can get in the way of discipline is that children who exhibit chronic misbehavior need instruction, not just punishment. Adults perceive these children as "living in their own little world" and believe that they "just don't care" about anything but what they want to do. Their bad behavior seems to demand punishment, so they are punished time and time again for the same negative behavior. The tendency then is to believe that if a five-minute timeout didn't work, maybe a ten-minute one will.

In school, it is common for these children to be sent to the office over and over even though their behavior never improves. In the meantime, the child or teen stays locked in a pattern of repetitive misbehavior. All this just makes the adults feel more frustrated. Feeling frustrated and powerless can cause most people to become angry, which, in turn, creates a vicious circle. The angrier the adult gets, the more these children act out. The punishment has gotten in the way of teaching the child new behavior.

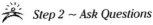 *Step 2 ~ Ask Questions*

At this point, everyone is operating out of the emotional centers of the brain, which makes problem solving difficult, if not impossible. Once this kind of cycle is in motion, it becomes essential that the adults take a psychological step backward. Adults have to get themselves into the *thinking* mode (the T part of the brain) and not give in to *feelings* of frustration. It is also necessary to move to the second aspect of asking questions for making discipline work. Ask questions for the purpose of assessment. The *thinking* mode allows the problem solving and assessment process to begin.

Ask Questions
For The Purpose Of Assessment

Questions are essential when dealing with chronic misbehavior. They are the keys to success with children or teens whose negative behavior continues after they have been punished repeatedly. Whether you are trying to figure out what is really going on with a child, or trying to teach the child to stay aware and take ownership of her *actions*, questions are necessary. Sometimes it is best to begin by asking yourself the following questions:

- What is going on with this child?
- Is there a certainty that this child *can* control this behavior?
- What is the child *feeling*?
- How does this child make me feel?
- What do I need when I feel like that?

Children and teens have an amazing ability to transfer their feelings into the adults around them. Many times, when I have been confused about what is going on internally with a child, I check in with myself and find out what I am feeling. Sometimes I am feeling frustrated, sometimes angry or disheartened. Inevitably, whatever I am feeling gives me a clue about what the child is feeling. Once you have a good idea about what they are feeling, you can figure out how to help them deal with those feelings in an acceptable fashion.

Keep in mind that young children rarely know how to describe what they are feeling. They can, however, if they get the proper help, be given the tools that will enable them to learn how their feelings can be described. In the beginning, they usually cannot answer questions such as: "What are you feeling?" or "How do you feel?" with an answer such as, "I feel stupid every day in this class because I can't do what the other kids can do." The best you can expect is something like "I don't know," or the most minimal response: "Bad!" Since emotions drive behavior, it is necessary to try to help children figure out what they are feeling. An excellent way to do that is to help them guess what they are feeling.

Ask questions such as:

- I wonder if you could be feeling frustrated because you have a hard time learning this stuff?
- If I give you a multiple choice of how you might be feeling will you tell me which word comes the closest to describing how you feel?
- Could you be feeling stressed, angry, confused?
- Tell me, if this feeling were an animal, what would it be?

There is a multitude of ways to get the feelings identified. I often show children, and some adults, a chart with feeling words and faces that express the feelings and let them point to the one that is the closest to the feeling they are having. This almost always works. I have tried all of the above strategies. It really depends on the age of the child. All have worked well. Being creative helps. I recommend that you never hesitate to help with a guess. Even if a person, child or adult has a good idea of what they are feeling, it does not mean that they can necessarily articulate the words. Your guess could help them find the words.

The point of asking questions about feelings is to help the child or teen develop a plan to handle the feelings in an acceptable way that will keep them out of trouble. The ultimate goal of discipline is to teach children an alternative, more effective way to handle themselves. Asking questions and seeking answers helps adults find out what children need to be taught in order to change their behavior. Punishment only teaches them that the behavior is not acceptable. Discipline teaches them what to do to ensure acceptable behavior in the future.

That is why the most important question for an adult to ask is:

What can I teach this child that will help him do what is expected of him the next time?

One mother was committed to making sure that her son would behave properly in school every day. She was a single parent who was determined that her son would respect the rules of the school and get a good education. Nevertheless, day after day the boy got in trouble. The teacher would call and complain and, day after day, the mother would punish her son severely. Still, the boy got into trouble. The mother finally asked me, "What can I do? I keep punishing him and he just keeps doing it!" My response was, "Start asking questions."

It was essential for this mother and her son's teacher to try to figure out what *feelings* were driving his behavior. What did the child need to keep himself from getting into trouble all the time? Given the consistency of the mother's response, and her determination that the boy would behave properly, there was a good possibility that this boy was experiencing some neurological or emotional problem. If true, restraining himself would be almost impossible. They needed those answers before an effective behavior change plan could be developed.[1]

Too often adults jump to conclusions about why children do what they do, and how much the child is able to help himself. It is sometimes hard for adults to believe that a child or teen may not be

---

[1] See *The ABC's Workbook: Creating a Behavior Change Plan That Works*, Divinyi, 2001.

able to change his or her behavior. Sometimes there may even be a need for medical intervention. There is almost always some reluctance on the part of adults to accept that a child may need medication to help him stay mentally focused or physically still long enough to concentrate. No one wants to medicate a child. Yet, there are thousands and thousands of children who can have infinitely more success in school and in life with the help of a little medical support.

People are always saying to me, "We didn't need medication when we were young." "Our parents just told us what to do, and we did it." While this is true for most of us, it is also true that the world has indeed changed enormously in the last 30-40 years. This includes the way children are being raised, the environment they live in and the way they play, to name a few. Any and all of these factors, and many more, can have an impact on the development of a child's brain. It just doesn't work well to assume that today's children will be "the way we were." There is little about the world today that is similar to the world in which most of us adults grew up.

Today, an increasing number of children experience neurological disorders. It is always best to seek expert assistance to determine if the child's refusal to respond to rules and structure is willful. Can he obey when he wants to or does the child seem *unable* to do anything expected of him, even when he appears contrite *after* the fact, or sincerely intent on staying out of trouble? Even experts sometimes have to take awhile to make this determination. Beware of jumping to conclusions. It is counter-productive to punish children for something they cannot control.

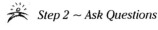

A Note About Medication

Medication for behavior difficulties is only one option for treating chronic misbehavior. At times, it is a possibility that should be seriously considered. A thorough assessment and evaluation by a well-trained professional is the first step in making this decision. Once a child is placed on medicine, it is essential that there be close medical supervision of the effects of the medicine. Sometimes the desired effect only happens after several different medications or dosages have been tried. Be sure to ask your doctor all of the questions you might have, particularly what side effects can be expected and how you will know whether or not the medicine is working. Questions, questions and more questions!

This is not meant to be a defense of medication for difficult behavior, nor is it a suggestion to rush to the conclusion that a particular child's problem can be solved with medication. Most responsible parents are not comfortable about giving children medicine that affects the brain. However, many parents do not know that when properly diagnosed and prescribed, medication can make a great deal of difference for some children. When nothing seems to be working with a child or teenager, and none of the questions you ask seem to have a reasonable answer, then a thorough medical evaluation is a good first step. This may help get to the root of the problem and get the child's behavior redirected.

However necessary and helpful it may be, though, medicine is not a substitute for discipline. Children who need medication to help with control of their behavior usually also need help learning how to handle their feelings and impulses. The effects of medicine only make it possible for children to control some of their own behavior. Medication does not teach them the techniques for developing the internal control they need to operate without intense supervision at all times.

Many children who get labeled a "discipline problem" need to be taught coping skills, or problem solving skills, or even thinking skills. As mentioned before, there is often an assumption that the child knows what to do and just doesn't want to do it. However, it is one thing for the child to know the rule of staying in their seat, or getting to class on time. It is another thing again to know what a person needs to do when they feel like getting out of their seat, or to know what they need to do to get to class on time.

Asking Questions About Public School

I hear these questions quite often: "Shouldn't the teacher or the school have to be responsible for making my child behave? Why should I have to constantly help them do their job?" Another comment I hear from parents is, "The teacher should understand that my child cannot help himself!" These are not realistic expectations for public school teachers. Many children need things that public schools have a difficult time providing. Some of the needs that children with chronic behavior difficulties have are: Quiet, tight structure, safety from threats, safety from humiliation, harassment or embarrassment, one-on-one attention, physical exercise and frequent movement, or alternative teaching styles.

Public schools have an enormous challenge trying to meet the individual needs of all students. The system is designed to meet most of the educational needs of the majority of students. It is not designed to address the basic unmet emotional needs that many children bring to school, nor is it designed to meet the needs of children with neurological or emotional disorders. However, feelings and needs drive behavior. Parents and teachers can work together to discover the emotions and needs that are prompting the child's difficult behavior. Such a collaborative effort greatly improves the chance that the child can be taught a new and better way to deal with those feelings and needs. Positive behavior change can then occur.

Some of the questions that parents and teachers can ask are:

- What is happening in the environment that might be contributing to the negative behavior?
- Are there places or people with whom this child has had no problem?
- What skill does the child need to learn in order to cope with the demands of the school environment?
- Who can help teach that skill to the child?

Teachers have difficulty managing this process without the support of parents, and visa versa. It takes a team of well-informed adults to teach (discipline) a child effectively enough that they can learn new behavior. Ideally parents and educators can work together toward this end. However, either parents or teachers can ask the questions and seek the answers needed to help the child without the support of the other. The ultimate goal is to determine how one can help this child learn a better way to manage his emotions. Too often, educators and parents believe that punishment is the answer to all behavior difficulties. It is not. Asking questions is the key to effective discipline.

Teach Children And Teens To Ask Questions

Asking both the child and yourself questions takes practice. It is not the usual way we deal with children. Habits, however, come with repetition, and asking questions is no exception. The more you do this the more comfortable it will become, especially when you see what a difference it will make. Another good thing about getting into the habit of asking questions is that it becomes the foundation for teaching children to ask themselves questions. Children and teens need to learn to question their own behavior.

They need to be able to say to themselves:

- What am I feeling?
- What am I doing?

- What do I need to do now?
- What will happen in the future if I do what I feel like doing now?

Once they are familiar with the concept of self-reflection and self-observation, they will become more able to control their own behavior. Teaching children self-control is one of the ultimate goals of good parenting.

Summary

Children are not always aware of what they are doing at a given time. They can be very unconscious of their behavior. It is difficult for children to control what for them is unconscious behavior. A first step in helping them pay attention to what they are doing is to bring it to their attention by asking questions. Ask them questions such as, "What are you doing?" and "What do you need to be doing?" This approach teaches them to self-observe. Self-observation is a learned skill, and is the first step in teaching self-control.

Teaching children to self-observe helps them take ownership of their behavior, which is the beginning of teaching them to be responsible for their own actions. Frequently, adults spend a good deal of time telling a child to stop or pay attention to what they are doing. Asking questions is more effective than merely telling them what they should or should not do. It requires them to focus on their behavior and become self-aware, rather than relying on adults to control their behavior.

When children have more ownership in the rules for behavior, they are more likely to cooperate with those rules. It is helpful to ask children if they can agree to the standards of behavior that are necessary for everyone. Once they have agreed, then adults can remind them of the proper standards by asking, "What was our agreement?" This teaches children to recognize that all rules are in place for a reason, and it allows them to recognize that obeying

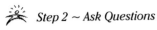

rules is their responsibility, not the responsibility of the adult in charge.

Once children have been taught to recognize when they are doing something unacceptable, and to take ownership of what they are doing, adults can then re-direct them to what they should be doing. Asking questions puts the focus on the proper behavior and prompts the child to do the right thing. It is best to keep the focus on the behavior that you want from the child. Discipline teaches the child to do the right thing. Sometimes punishment can get in the way of discipline. Rushing to punishment for rule breaking or misbehavior sometimes takes the focus off the positive behavior that is required. When punishment is necessary, it is important to ask the child or teen questions about what they will need to do to keep from handling a similar situation in the same unacceptable way again.

When children do not learn alternative ways to handle a situation, and they get themselves into trouble, they can develop a pattern of chronic misbehavior. The key to stopping chronic misbehavior is asking questions. The first question needs to be, "What is going on with this child?" There is always a reason for chronic misbehavior, and that reason is usually related to unconscious *feelings* and needs that the child is acting out. When a pattern of chronic misbehavior develops, children can seem to become immune to punishment.

When this happens, it is important for adults to ask questions about what emotions may be prompting the child's behavior. A child who is suffering from a neurological disorder or some form of mental illness, including depression, may not be able to control his or her own behavior. Repeatedly punishing a child for behavior that he may not be able to control creates feelings of intense frustration for both the child and the adults who are charged with teaching them proper behavior. A thorough medical examination is the best way to determine what, if any, medical support the child will need to help him control his own behavior.

Finally, teaching children to ask themselves questions about their behavior helps teach them self-control. Even asking questions after the fact can help them understand why they did what they did, and what they need to do next time the same situation comes up. Asking questions is a highly effective discipline and diagnostic tool.

Discipline That Works: 5 Simple Steps

STEP 3 TEACH SKILLS

The teaching component of disciplining a child is frequently overlooked or given little attention. Effective discipline requires adults to help children and teens develop the skills they need to keep themselves from repeating negative behavior. This means teaching them how to keep themselves from acting on emotions, how to think about consequences, and how to help themselves do the things they don't feel like doing. Some children develop these skills naturally through good parenting and healthy play. Many do not. This chapter discusses the process of how to teach children these skills.

Teach Children Coping Skills

Teaching children to use self-control means helping them develop coping skills and social skills. Coping skills are what we use to help ourselves deal with emotions. Most adults learned these skills in the process of maturation. They have learned ways to overcome an initial impulse or emotional reaction and get into the thinking mode before they act. On a good day, most of us know how to calm ourselves down or push ourselves to do things that we don't feel like doing. We know how to get along in a group, how to be polite and how to respect other people's space and property. These are the skills needed to move from the E (emotions) part of the brain to the T (thinking) part of the brain and on to appropriate A (action). Of course, we all have days when we fail to use the self-control or social skills that we know. More often than not, however, healthy adults can direct their own behavior, even when there may be situations that tempt them to lose control or shut down. Usually we are not conscious of these skills. We just use them without having to think about it.

Healthy adults can also problem-solve. They can reason out what to do in a difficult situation in order to help them cope when things get rough. Gaining a mastery of these skills is vitally important for keeping us on track and living a healthy and productive life. People who have not learned these skills tend to have chaotic or even tragic lives. That is why good parents are determined to teach their children manners and self-control.

The best way to do this is to personally model the behavior you desire from your children when loving, nurturing and disciplining them. However, even the best discipline, love and nurturing does not automatically develop children's coping or social skills. This is especially true if the adults around them do not model these behaviors for the children to see. It is alarming how many role models who do not have these skills are portrayed in the media. Children watch these people and learn how to *not* use self-control or basic courtesy and respect. This makes actively teaching these skills to children more important than ever. When adults stay focused upon teaching children coping skills, discipline becomes easier and more effective. An effective adult continually provides a child with step-by-step instructions for handling him or herself appropriately.

Ask Questions First

Sometimes it is not always clear what skills children need in order to learn. The tendency is to focus on the unacceptable behavior rather than on those things they need to learn or do. That is why it is important to determine what kind of skills a particular child needs in order to improve their behavior. Asking questions is the first step in this process.

When a child is acting inappropriately, the questions you ask will point toward the area of skills in which the child most needs to learn. For instance, when you ask a child about what he is doing, and the answer over and over again is "fighting," then clearly the child needs to learn how to control his temper. He needs to learn how to handle conflict without striking out inappropriately. What often happens, though, is that the adult takes the option of administering immediate punishment. Adults can make the mistake of thinking that it is the punishment itself that is doing the teaching, and then they wonder why the child keeps getting in trouble over and over again for the same thing. Some of us assume that the child "knows better." We presume that he just chooses not to do what he should do. Yes, punishment for fighting does teach the child that it is wrong to hit others. This is necessary and important for him to know. Beyond that, however, we soon see that it does not teach him any skills that will enable him to control his temper or avoid a fight in the future. Just because the child has been taught that fighting is wrong and against the rules, it does not follow that he knows how to calm himself down when he gets mad. He does not yet have the skills, the know-how, needed so that he can walk away from an unnecessary conflict.

These are skills that must be taught. They will need to be taught, sometimes repeatedly, if the child is going to learn how to keep from making the same mistakes over and over again. Teaching these skills means going over them with the child, letting the child practice what needs to be done next time, and getting him or her to agree to do the new behavior. Many children make the same mistakes repeatedly because they don't know what else to do. It never occurs to them that there are alternatives to striking out during an unhappy or frustrating moment. This simple method of presenting them with an alternative behavior is an excellent discipline tool. Why? It teaches. Even when punishment is necessary, reviewing the child's behavior and teaching him or her another way to handle the situation next time is true discipline. Discipline is teaching. Teaching skills makes discipline work.

There are a multitude of skills and strategies that children can be taught to help them learn how to change their own behavior. Teaching these skills simply requires adults to explain to children how to do these things, and help them practice doing it. Generally, self-control skills fall into one of two categories — *emotional coping skills* or *social skills*.

Emotional coping skills teach children how:

- To calm down when they are very angry or upset
- To use words instead of actions to express their feelings
- To follow rules they don't agree with or don't like
- To pay attention to other people's feelings
- To pay attention to other people's space
- To stay focused
- To stop when they don't feel like stopping
- To make themselves work, even when they don't feel like working
- To handle frustrations
- To handle disappointments
- To handle successes

Social skills teach children how:

- To respond to authority figures
- To work well with others
- To take turns
- To be courteous and respectful
- To be respectful even when others are rude
- To say "no" to peers
- To ask for help when they need it

These are only a few skills that children need to be taught when their behavior becomes difficult or unacceptable. Most of these skills require a child to move from emotions to thinking, to be able to go through the E-T-A (*emotions-thinking-action*) sequence instead of the E-A-T (*emotions-action-thinking*) sequence at the moment they need to make a good decision.

Children Learn At Play

Children also learn coping skills at play. Many of us learned to take turns and even control our tempers while we were playing with our friends. We learned that if you lost your cool, you wouldn't get to play again. We learned to work as a team. We even learned how to create a team of our own because everything wasn't organized for us. We played outside and used our imaginations and created strategies to outsmart our peers. Today's children often spend a large portion of their time in passive and solitary activities such as watching television or videos. Even computer games and Internet activities, which aren't totally passive, are nonetheless very solitary. It is hard to understand how children today can learn the kind of social and coping skills taught to previous generations. Today's children spend too much time in passive, solo activities.

Even a simple skill, like waiting for your turn, is something that has to be learned through interaction with others. When it comes to teaching children self-control, it is important to recognize

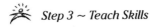

that they may not yet have learned even one of these simple skills. When they do not have even a basic awareness of these social coping skills, they tend to act inappropriately, get into trouble, and remain unaffected by punishment. That's why punishment needs to be coupled with skill building activities.

Set A Good Example

Sometimes adults can teach a child how to do things that they themselves cannot do. A swim coach, for example, can teach a swimmer to be a champion without being a champion herself. A mother can encourage her daughter to learn skills that she herself does not possess. However, it is almost impossible for someone to teach children self-control skills if the teaching adult does not have this capacity within himself or herself in the first place. This is how we all learn our first basic skills of walking and talking. We listen and watch the various demonstrations of others around us. It is also through demonstration that we learn how to handle our emotions and solve problems.

It is possible that some parents who do have self-control skills can still have a great deal of difficulty teaching them to their children. Teaching is sometimes harder than doing, and there are many factors that play into the learning process. Nonetheless, there is still a great potential for success if the parents are attuned to teaching their children. However, it is not likely that parents or adults who do not have the ability to control their own emotions and behavior will be able to teach these skills to the children in their lives. The good news is that it is never too late to learn emotional coping skills. Adults who are committed to the children in their care can still seek help in learning the emotional skills they want the children to learn. This requires adults to recognize that they need help and take action to get it. It also requires that adults be honest with themselves. This can be difficult, but it is not as difficult as struggling with self-control within themselves while at the same time trying to teach it to children.

Educate Children About How Their Brain Works

The first step in teaching children self-control skills is to teach them how their brain works. Both children and adults need to learn to understand their own behavior. We expect to teach children how their bodies work. As they get older they are educated about what different organs of the body do and how they work together to keep the body running. Rarely do we teach children to understand how their brains work. Teaching the simple *E-T-A model* of the brain helps children learn, in the simplest way possible, to recognize the difference between *feeling* and *thinking*. That is the beginning of teaching them to take charge of their *emotions*, their *thinking* and their *actions*.

I have taught this simple model of the brain to children of all ages and in many different settings. Most children are interested in learning about themselves. When children are toddlers their brains are not developed enough to control themselves. They are also too young to teach even this simple explanation of the brain. That is why they have to be watched carefully until they are able to make judgments and respond to commands. They can, however, be taught to recognize when they are sad or mad or tired, or any number of other emotions.

By the time they are five or six, most children can understand a simple explanation of how their brain works. Oftentimes, this simple explanation can help children or teenagers make sense of their own "crazy" behavior. This is the beginning step of teaching them how to control their behavior. When they recognize that even very smart people can do dumb things if their emotions get out of control, children can then be taught the skills they need to master to move from *E*motions, to *T*hinking and on to appropriate *A*ction.

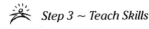

Teaching the E-T-A Model

The following is a simplified explanation that can be used to teach children the E-T-A model of brain function. (The language level can be adjusted up or down with the child's age.)

The brain is a very complicated organ. It is easiest to understand if we think about how it works in the simplest way. Here's how it works:

Different parts of the brain do different things.

It is sort of like a big department store where one part of the store has clothes and another part has towels and another part has things for babies. They are all located in the same store.

One part of the brain makes it possible for us to feel. I call it the *E* for *E*motions. It lets us feel happy or sad or mad. It is a very important part of the brain because it lets us feel danger and tells us if something is wrong so that we can protect ourselves. It is also important because it makes it possible for us to feel good and glad to be alive.

A second part of the brain makes it possible for us to think. I call it the *T* for *T*hinking. It is the part of the brain that lets us figure out how to solve a problem.

A third part of the brain lets us take action. It is the *A* for *A*ction. This is the part of the brain that decides what we are going to do.

Between these parts of the brain are *bridges* or cables, similar to phone lines, or aisles in our big department store, which make it possible for all the parts of the brain to connect and talk to each other.

There is another thing that the brain helps us do, but it is not in a special part. It is just something the brain can do if all the *bridges* in the brain are working right. That is the ability to think about the future. This is a very important task for a brain to do because it allows us to think about how things might work out for us in the future. It lets me remember that if I do something my *emotions* want me to do, even if I know it is wrong, I might get into trouble later. That would not be good.

Even when these parts of the brain are working together in the right way, we can still have an *emotion* that makes us want to do something we know is wrong. However, if we get across the *bridge* into the *thinking* part of the brain, we will begin to think, "This may not be a good idea." Then we think about what could happen in the future if we go ahead and do what we feel like doing. We can then decide to not do what we feel like doing and take the right *action* instead. This is how our brain works when everything is working the way it is supposed to.

Sometimes things get out of order in our brains. This is most likely to happen if we are having really big *feelings*. If our *feelings* get very intense, sometimes the bridge from the *E, emotions,* to the *T, thinking,* can go out, and the next thing you know, we are doing something strictly because we feel like it. It may be something we wouldn't do if we were *thinking*. When the "bridge is out" between the *E* and the *T*, we stop *thinking*, or if we do think, we do not go on to think about how the *actions* we take will affect our future.

That is why it is so important to pay attention to how we are *feeling*. If we aren't careful, we can do things without *thinking* and that usually doesn't work very well for us.

* * *

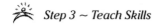

There are many ways to explain this simple concept, and you can use the words and metaphors that you think the child or teen will best understand. The important thing is to take the time to teach children the difference between *feeling* and *thinking*. Teach them to recognize that when their *actions* are driven by their emotions it can get them into trouble.

Review The Unacceptable Behavior With The Child

It is in the nature of being a child to make mistakes. Childhood is one big learning process, and expecting children or teens to never make a mistake is unfair to anyone. Mistakes will happen. Children even need to learn that they ought not to expect themselves to be perfect, just smart. They need to be smart enough to learn from mistakes. The goal is to help them learn something from the mistakes they make. That is why it is so important to discuss mistakes with children. Discussing a mistake is not the same as criticizing or berating a child for making a mistake. That is counterproductive. It just makes the child feel stupid or hurt or angry.

The goal of good discipline is to get the child into the *thinking* mode so that he will not find himself isolated in the *feeling* mode alone. Talking about unacceptable behavior is a review process. The goal of discussing a child's behavior with him is to review *how* his behavior came to make the mistake. We need to help children consider what they need to do to keep from making that mistake again. It is an essential part of healthy discipline. It helps the child think about his *actions*. It is far more productive to get children to *think* rather than *feel*. If *feelings* are the only tool that a child has to work with to express himself, he will soon be far afield from where anyone wants him to be.

Determine The Missing Skill

Going through the review process means asking the child or teen questions about what happened *before* the time their mistake got them into trouble. When they misbehave, especially when they commit similar acts over and over, ask them to reflect on what happened. This is not the time to focus on the *sequence* of the problem event itself, but rather the things that led up to the event. Ask questions. Be careful not to jump to conclusions about what happened. The goal is to find out what prompted the behavior, not just what they did wrong. Ask all kinds of questions:

- How do you think this happened?
- What were you *feeling* before it happened?
- What were you *thinking*?
- What did you feel after it happened?
- Did you feel smart, dumb, strong, or stupid?
- Where were you when it happened?
- When did you feel OK?
- When were things going OK?

Now focus on the sequence of events:

- What happened from the time things were OK to when you got in trouble?
- Do you know what you could have done differently?
- What do you think you could do next time you have this *feeling* so that you can stay out of trouble?

The answer to these questions will help you determine what skills the child needs to learn. For instance, if they have no clue as to how or why things happened, then they will need your help to walk them through what did happen. Then they can learn how to make the necessary connections to figure things out in the future. It is possible to teach them to self-observe after the fact. Getting them to acknowledge each step in the process that got them into trouble does it. If they do not know how they feel, you can help them figure it out.

Try guessing. Say, "Could you have been *feeling...*?" Asking where they were and when they felt OK can be very informative. It can give you a clue about what triggered the troublesome events. Let's use an example to demonstrate how the above questions and answers can reveal the skills a child needs to learn.

After a fight in the hall at school:

Adult:	How do you think this happened?
Child:	I don't know.
Adult:	What were you *feeling* before it happened?
Child:	Mad. He shoved me first.
Adult:	What were you *thinking*?
Child:	I don't know.
Adult:	What did you feel after it happened?
Child:	Scared because I was going to get into trouble.
Adult:	Besides scared, did you feel smart, dumb, strong, or stupid?
Child:	He just makes me mad.
Adult:	Where were you when it happened?
Child:	In the hall.
Adult:	When did you feel OK?
Child:	In Ms. Green's class.
Adult:	When were things going OK?
Child:	Before the bell rang.

Now focus on the sequence of events:

Adult:	What happened from the time things were OK to when you got in trouble?

Child:	Ms. Brown yelled at me in front of everybody when we went into the hall.
Adult:	So you got in a fight because you were mad at Ms. Brown.
Child:	Yes, I guess so.
Adult:	What do you think you could do next time you are mad at a teacher instead of fighting with one of your classmates?
Child:	Well, I don't know.
Adult:	Maybe you could just tell someone you are mad. You wouldn't have to show how mad you are. If you just say it, you will feel less mad and won't have to hit someone. Do you think you could try that next time?
Child:	Yeah, I guess so. Maybe I could tell Ms. Green. She's nice.
Adult:	That's a good idea. Then you won't be getting in trouble for fighting just because another teacher yelled at you.

Initially, the issue with this boy was a case of fighting with his peers. After a question and answer dialogue it became clear that he did not know how to express anger at an adult. He took his anger out on the nearest and easiest target: a fellow student. If the discipline for fighting had only focused on the fight itself, the boy would not have had an opportunity to learn how to handle a situation when he is angry with an adult. Most children don't know an appropriate way to handle anger with adults. If we don't teach them, they will continue to express their anger inappropriately.

The goal of asking questions is to pin down exactly what the child needs to learn.

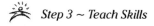

If a child gets in trouble for:	He needs to learn this:
Bumping into other children	How to recognize people's personal space
Getting mad because he has to take turns	How to calm down and wait
Hitting	How to use words instead of *actions* to express *feelings*
Making fun of someone in a mean way	How to pay attention to other people's *feelings*

Whatever the trouble, there is a corresponding skill that the child can learn to keep from getting in trouble again. The problem is that most of the time the adult-child interaction stops right at that point of discussing what happened and what was wrong about it. The discussion rarely goes to the next step in helping the child actually learn a new skill.

How To Teach A Skill

All it takes to teach young people a coping or social skill is to explain to them how to use the skill. Then explain that you want them to do this the next time the same situation comes up. Make them practice the skill. If you are teaching them how to calm themselves down by breathing or talking to themselves, demonstrate the skill for them. Show them what you would do to calm yourself down. Then get them to do it for you or with you. End the conversation with an agreement that they will indeed do this the next time.

I have had the following dialogue with many young teens who have gotten into trouble for fighting. Here's an example of teaching a skill:

Adult:	OK, you lost your temper because the boy shoved you.
Teen:	Yeah. He didn't have a right to touch me!

Adult:	True. He didn't. But you can let him know that he doesn't have a right to touch you without hitting him back. Next time this happens, this is what I want you to do. Say, nice and loud — you don't have to yell — but you can say it so he knows you really mean it, "Keep your hands off me. You don't have a right to touch me." Use words! You can't go around hitting anyone who touches. You can stand up for your rights without hitting someone. OK, now we are going to practice. Pretend you just got shoved. Say what I said. Say it like you mean it.
Teen:	*(In a low voice)* Keep your hands off me. You don't have a right to touch me.
Adult:	Say it again, like I did.
Teen:	*(Louder)* Keep your hands off me!
Adult:	That's better. Now can we agree that this is what you are going to do next time?
Teen:	What if he shoves me again?
Adult:	Then you say it again and you back up. You don't have to sound scared, and if he doesn't stop, then walk away.
Teen:	He'll come after me.
Adult:	Then you just keep saying, "Stop it." Then you come get me. You are probably going to feel like hitting him. Stay in the *T* part of your brain so that you can remember that if you hit him, he will be in control of the situation and you might get in as much trouble as he

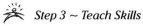

does. The resource officer won't necessarily believe that he shoved you first. I
don't want to see you get suspended
because this boy is looking for trouble.
Remember, any time someone can
make you lose your cool, they have
control over you. You keep the control.
If you stay in the *T* part of your brain,
you will figure out what to do. I am
confident you can do this. This boy is
not worth it. Keep saying to yourself,
"Stay in the *T*." It will help you keep
control of your emotions.

This example may seem silly to some, but when a teenager
hits another, it requires a disciplinary action. To discipline is to teach.
Some young teens have no adult teaching them *how* to do the right
thing. Someone has to show them how it is done. They may not get
it the first time, but that will give the adult an opportunity to review
what happened and what should have happened. Punishing this
teenager for breaking the rules may be necessary, but it will not
automatically teach him a different way to handle a difficult situation.

Typically, teaching a skill is not as challenging as the above
example. It can be as simple as the following example:

Parent:	The teacher says you are constantly interrupting her when she is talking. Is that true?
Child: ·	Yes, but she never calls on me.
Parent:	That can be very frustrating, but blurting out all the time is not the way to handle frustrations. You need to find another

	way. Can you think of something else to do?
Child:	Raise my hand.
Parent:	That would be good, but we need to figure out something for you to do when the teacher doesn't call on you. What if you write your question or answer down and give it to the teacher later. If that doesn't work just put your hand over your mouth. I've had to do that at times when I wanted to say something when I wasn't supposed to. Can you do that?
Child:	Yes sir, I guess so.
Parent:	Ok. I am going to be checking with the teacher.

Acknowledge Feelings First

Be sure to acknowledge the child's feelings once they have been able to state them. Acknowledgement of another person's feelings is not the same as agreeing that they were entitled to act on the feelings as they did. It is simply an expression of compassion or understanding and helps keep the child from getting defensive or angrier. In any dialogue, when a person becomes defensive, there is little chance of getting them to the problem-solving mode. Notice, in the above dialogue, the parent expressed empathy and understanding by stating that it can be frustrating not to be called on by the teacher. Empathy and understanding are great tools for helping people of any age to get from the E (emotions) to the T (thinking) part of their brain. It is necessary for both the child and the adult to be in the T part of the brain if a skill is to be taught.

Teaching a skill is simply a matter of giving the child a plan to help him out of trouble. This basic strategy will go a long way to-

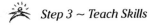

wards helping a child do something different the next time. This process rarely happens when parents and other adults are disciplining a child or teen. Yet, training is the foundation of discipline.

Teach "Boring Skills"

One of the coping skills that I have observed to be missing for many children and adolescents is the ability to cope with boredom. Children today are accustomed to high-stimulus entertainment. They watch television from extremely young ages. Television changes images every few seconds. Computer games are very high-stimulus. Children get used to fast-paced distractions and have a difficult time when they are required to just sit and listen or, heaven forbid, study.

It can be very helpful with these children to teach them how to cope with boredom. It isn't easy. However, sheer boredom gets more children and adolescents into trouble than almost anything else. Many times I have seen extremely bright kids get failing grades in a class that bores them. The reality is that life can be boring at times. Many of the tasks we have to accomplish are boring. We have to do them, however, in order to get the opportunity to do the kind of things we like to do. I have said to teens that I have worked with, "You are going to need to learn 'boring skills.'" Boring skills help us cope with boredom. It is not OK to get in trouble or fail just because you're bored."

Some of the strategies that I have suggested to cope with boredom are:

> **In class:** Doodle; get up and move whenever possible; talk to yourself; say "focus" to yourself when your mind wanders; count down the time you have to stay focused. Imagine pictures of the words the teacher is saying.
>
> **Doing homework:** Listen to music; watch TV. (Note: Sometimes this strategy can backfire, but many children do get more work accomplished when they have to keep their attention on two things at once.

I can't explain this, but I know that it is true.) Work short periods, take a *brief* break, and work again. Give yourself a reward for finishing in a certain time. Do it sooner rather than later so that you can look forward to doing something fun afterward.

Doing chores: Play energetic music. Break a big task down into small ones. Use head phones to listen to your favorite music. Give yourself a treat when you finish. Make a game of it.

Nike ® Issues

This is my personal favorite. When something just has to be done, even if it is boring or just not fun, it can help to identify the task as a "Nike Issue." Nike Issues are "Just Do It" issues. They may be miserable or boring or just plain hard but they have to be done. Nike Issues are also "no argument" issues. There are many things an adult can and will negotiate with a child. Children are masterful negotiators, but teaching young people when it is and is not okay to negotiate is an important part of discipline. Labeling the non-negotiable tasks is a way to teach children discernment. It can also save a great deal of wear and tear on you. Not only that, it can be surprising how much more children are willing to get something done once an adult acknowledges that it may be boring or unpleasant. When I tell kids that something is a "Nike Issue," I am letting them know two things: First, that I understand why they don't want to do it, and second, that I am not willing to argue or negotiate.

Summary

Teaching children and teens coping skills and social skills is the crux of effective discipline. Parents and adults must teach children the specific skills they need in order to help them change the behavior that keeps getting them in trouble. Children spend much more time in passive and solitary activities than in years past. Children today often do not develop skills for dealing with others or for coping with their own emotions. Their interpersonal interactions are far more limited today than they were; in past years almost all of a child's playtime was spent in physical and outdoor activities with other children.

Children also learn from role models. There is a wide variety of coping and social skills that children will not develop unless adult role models are coupled with instruction. Children are surrounded on a daily basis, through exposure to television, movies, and the Internet, with role models for improper and impulsive behavior. It is necessary for adults to model the skills they want to teach. Discipline for inappropriate behavior must include step-by-step instruction for proper behavior.

Adults must take the time to discuss the specific details of the events leading up to misdeeds. This includes the *emotions* the child or teen was experiencing at the time, not just what they were *thinking*. This information will help adults determine the specific skills that must be taught in order to keep the child from making the same mistakes again.

One of the most important things children and teens need to learn is how their brain works. They need to understand that the brain is a compartmentalized organ. One part of the brain governs *emotion, E,* another *thinking, T* and another *action, A.* Communication "bridges" connect these areas of the brain. These "bridges" allow the brain's *thinking* part to communicate with the brain's *feeling* part. These connections will help people make a good decision about what to do with *feelings* and impulses.

Making good decisions is also linked to the brain's ability to consider things that will happen in the future. When the brain's "bridges" aren't working well, *emotions* can cause people to do things without *thinking* about consequences for their acts. Teaching children and teens the *E-T-A* model of the brain will help them learn to pay attention to their *feelings* and *think* before they act.

Skill building is teaching children exactly what to do when they *feel* like doing something that will get them in trouble. Children and teens do not necessarily know what alternative behaviors are available at a critical moment, even if they are aware that their *action*s will cause them trouble. Punishment does not teach them an alternative behavior. Teaching a different way, through description, how to handle a situation, and practicing that skill or strategy with them, will give them a much better opportunity to learn new behavior options and eventually change negative behavior.

.

Discipline That Works: 5 Simple Steps

STEP  4 REPEAT SHORT PHRASES

Repeating rules, commands, directions and expectations is a necessary component of the discipline process. The brain needs repetition in order to encourage the formation of good habits. However, parents and teachers can become very frustrated when they have to tell children the same things over and over. Not only that, children, especially teens, become quite proficient at "tuning out." This chapter gives guidelines for determining when and how repetition is helpful and when it is not.

The brain needs a certain amount of repetition in order for a particular behavior to become a habit. This is the reason that children and teens sometimes need to be told the same thing over and over. They need this repetition because their young brains are still in the process of developing new neuro-pathways. These new brain pathways will eventually allow them to act appropriately, on their own initiative, without the need for adult prompting.

Since the goal of healthy discipline is to teach new and proper behavior, it is often necessary to find ways to remind children of what they need to be doing. We need to do this in a manner that does not cause them to tune out our words. We also want to avoid becoming frustrated or angry ourselves. Most parents have found themselves saying, "Haven't I told you that before?" or, "I get so tired saying the same things over and over!" Neither of these oft-repeated phrases seems to have much impact in terms of getting the child or teenager to respond in a better manner. They are more expressions of exasperation than they are positive verbal behavior prompts. A quick expression of exasperation is understandable, but it does not accomplish the goal of helping youngsters develop healthy behavior. It is the verbal behavior prompt that children need.

There are two things that can help with this trying situation. The first is to use *short directive phrases* over and over instead of giving long (or short) lectures. The second is to stick to the "Two Sentence Rule." Quit talking after you say two sentences[1]. Verbal prompting is often necessary to get a child or teen to do the things they need to do. It does not, however, need to be done with lots of words. In fact, the more words that adults use to get a child going in the right direction, the more likely it is that the child *will tune out or ignore them.*

---

[1] Thanks to Sandra Halperin, Ph.D. for her excellent coaching and teaching me the "Two Sentence Rule."

Discipline That Works: 5 Simple Steps

Sorry, Mom. I didn't hear you call the first four times.

Jerry Spurgeon / larissaholland.com

Repeat Short Phrases

Keep in mind that the goal of directing a child to do something is to teach them to do it so that in the future they do not need you to personally guide them. Combining short repetitive and positive phrases with a particular skill that needs to be learned helps a child or adolescent form the habit of internally reminding themselves. The more positive the repeated phrases are, the more likely the brain will develop healthy and acceptable behavior. The brain prefers positive messages to negative messages. It is better to use phrases that tell a child to do something right rather than tell them to stop doing something wrong. We have all noted in our own lives that it is more effective to tell ourselves we should "eat healthy" or "think thin," rather than say, "don't eat that chocolate!"

The more we tell ourselves *not* to do something, the more we want to do it. Children are especially prone to this characteristic of human nature. Children are used to hearing "stop" messages. Such messages have a tendency to become routine and consequently are "tuned out" quite easily. To help them develop positive behavior, it is necessary that they hear "go" messages repeatedly. A "go" message is simply a verbal directive that tells them what they need to do, rather than what *not* to do. Once they have heard these positive messages several times, they will begin to repeat the phrases to themselves. This process will eventually get them to do what is necessary without outside prompting. This may take some time, but it does keep the focus on encouraging the child to think about what he *is* doing, or *needs* to do, rather than what he should *not* be doing. It also has the added benefit of not requiring so much energy from parents or other adults.

Short phrases need to be directive, positive and focused on a specific behavior that the child or teen needs to learn. They only need to be two or three words. Sometimes, even one single word will do. These words need to remind the child of a self-control skill or a coping tool. These short phrases serve as prompts, and become verbal "road signs" for young people.

Repeat the phrases in a directive and positive tone of voice. If your tone changes from calm and firm to angry or sharp, the child is more likely to have an emotional reaction rather than a thinking response. The goal is to trigger the thinking part of the brain, not the emotional part. When adults become emotional, children see this and become emotional as well. When children become emotional, they stop thinking clearly. The goal is to get them to think, or resume thinking. So, as you carefully choose the phrases to use, and repeat them as often as necessary, remember to maintain a firm and positive tone.

Do not use any of the directive phrases you choose in conjunction with a comment about the child's personal character or personal potential. Likewise, you should not comment about a child's current inability to act correctly on his or her own initiative. A *short* phrase is *short*. It stands alone. It may be necessary to repeat the same phrase twice in succession, or even repeatedly throughout a given day. To get the desired result, these directive phrases cannot be attached to other words, lectures or comments. If they do become so attached, they lose their power as a behavior prompt and will not be successful as an effective discipline tool.

This is a typical parent directive at homework time:

Parent: Josh, get back to work. You are not going out to play until this homework is done. If you would just keep at it you'd get it over with. You always make this harder than it is. Just get busy and don't get up until it is done.

Usually the child has a lot to say in response to the above directive. Then more time is spent struggling and more words are exchanged and less homework is accomplished.

An alternative is:

Parent: Josh, stay on task!

or

Parent: Josh, focus!

For the second example to work, the child has to have been trained to understand what the short phrases mean and what he is expected to do when he hears them.

For example (*Parent/Teacher*):

P/T: From now on, when I say, "stay on task" that will be your reminder to get back to work and finish what you are doing. It can work even better if you say the same thing to yourself, "Stay on task." This way we don't always have to discuss something every time you get

distracted from your work. It's easy to
get distracted but you can bring your
attention back by using this simple
phrase. "Stay on task" is your cue to
remind yourself that you need to finish
a particular job. Can you do this?

Any time you are trying to teach children new behavior, re-member to ask for an *agreement* from them as to what exactly they are going to do. Agreements imply and assign more responsibility to them for accomplishing what they are expected to do. They rein-force within the child that he or she has power over his or her own behavior. In the above example, if Josh should respond with all the reasons why he is off-task, the parent just repeats the short phrase, which reminds Josh of what he needs to do. This takes less energy from the parent. It also helps the child by reminding him of what he needs to do. It is not a process of reminding him of what he is doing wrong.

Choose The Phrases Carefully

Decide what phrases will work best for the situation. Keep in mind what the child needs to learn. Different phrases work best in different situations. In the above example, "Stay on task" is a good phrase for teachers and parents to use, especially with children with attention deficit disorder. These children are very distractible. Even when they are taking medication to help them stay focused, they still need to learn skills for helping themselves pull their attention back from wherever it has wandered. "Stay on task," repeated as necessary, helps these students bring their attention back to the behavior issue at hand.

I have used this phrase with myself many times. I am easily distractible when I am doing a task I don't particularly enjoy, such as paying bills or almost any kind of paperwork.

I find it more effective for me to say to myself:

"Stay on task, Joyce."…

Rather than giving myself an internal lecture such as:

"You need to keep at this and get it done. You've let it go too long, so just stay at it. You have to get this done now because you need to get back to that manuscript you want to finish."

The next thing you know, I'm *thinking* about the manuscript rather than the paperwork I need to do. Sometimes my own internal lectures get me distracted rather than calling me back to task. When I use the phrase, "Stay on task," I can pull my attention back to the business at hand. This is what you are trying to accomplish with children: to get them to develop internalized behavior management skills.

It takes practice to develop these skills. That is why it helps so much for adults to *repeat* the short phrases. Adults then become coaches in a manner similar to athletic coaches. Good coaches remind their athletes of what they already know with either (short) phrases or (short) hand signals. These short phrases can become power phrases in that they have the power to help build brain pathways that are the foundation of new behavior habits. Adults can create their own phrases to suit the situation. Once a phrase is chosen, explain its meaning to the child or adolescent. Be specific about what they are supposed to do when they hear the phrase.

The following are examples of short phrases and how they can be used to prompt new behavior.

Power Phrases

"Stay on task."
Use this phrase to remind children to bring their attention back to a given task or chore.

"Focus."
This is a one-word prompt for getting a child to pay attention. Direct the child to look at and listen carefully to a

speaker. It can also direct them to concentrate on a task that needs careful attention.

"Do it the first time."

Children and teens should be expected to obey the *first* time they are told. Often they do not. Explain that these power phrases will remind them that they are expected to do what they are told *right now*, without discussion or pleas such as, "Can't I do it later?" When you repeat this phrase they are reminded that they are dealing with a non-negotiable "Nike Issue."

"Listen up."

This phrase can cut through the noise and chatter that are usually going on when children are around. Tell them this phrase means "stop talking and listen right now." Repeating this phrase, instead of yelling over the din, takes less energy. It also signals to *do* something — to "listen" — as opposed to *not do* something — not talk or not make noise.

"Be kind."

This is a short version of the Golden Rule. There are very few things that children need to learn that are more important than how to treat others kindly. Sometimes it is necessary to be clear and specific about the definition of kindness. Kindness means helping others, being mindful of their feelings so they do not feel bad or hurt, and being okay with them even when they are different than you.

Tell children that when you use the "Be kind" phrase you expect them to check in with themselves and make sure they are doing one of these three things — *helping*, being *gentle* with someone else's feelings or being *tolerant* of someone who is different.

This is a powerful phrase. You can explain that you may not be able to keep people outside of your authority from being hurtful to others, but you can make sure that everyone in your family or classroom is treated kindly and with respect.

"Use words."

This phrase means to *say what you are feeling* instead of acting it out. It means using words to deal with a conflict instead of hitting or throwing things or yelling. Explain to children that they must *use words to say* they are mad or upset or agitated or nervous or whatever they may be *feeling* or *thinking*. This phrase can be used every time a conflict develops between one or more children or teens. Tell them that they have to sit down and talk about the conflict. Help them find the words if they can't come up with them on their own. You can say, "Sit down and tell him what makes you mad. Then he will tell you." Once you have done this several times, you will be able to say simply, "Use words," and that will be their signal to engage the verbal part of their thinking brain.

The tendency when children get into conflicts, especially physical conflicts, is to punish them for fighting. This may be necessary, but the punishment needs to be paired with the discipline of having to fight in a socially acceptable fashion, using words to express feelings and differences. Many children do not have this skill because they have not been taught. Teach them.

Of course, to "Use words" means to use appropriate and effective words, not mere curse words. Cursing has become so common in our culture that children are exposed to it everywhere. Young people need to be taught that, even if cursing has become common in everyday life, it still possesses zero problem-solving qualities in the context of this discussion. To put it most simply, it is ineffective. Teaching children to use the right words will increase the effectiveness of any and all of their communications.

These simple phrases, repeated over and over, are discipline tools. They teach. They also save time and energy. There are many more examples of short phrases that work as teaching tools. We use short phrases automatically. "Be careful." "Buckle up." "Be quiet." Choosing to use a particular phrase, explaining the phrase and the response that is expected following the use of this phrase, is common for adults who are tending to children. What is not as common is choosing new phrases for the purpose of teaching specific skills. I have used this technique many times, in many settings, and am always impressed with its effectiveness. It takes the place of lectures and scolding or, in worst-case scenarios, ranting and raving.

Stick To The "Two Sentence Rule"

Sometimes we cannot say what needs to be said in one or two short sentences. Sometimes it is necessary and important to explain a decision that has been made to a child or teen. However, explaining something does not mean justifying, nor does it mean arguing or pleading with the child to agree that your decision is fair or reasonable. Many times, adults want children or teens to do what they are told *and* like it as well. This really isn't fair. It is enough that they do what they are told to do. Give them permission to not like it. That means they can gripe, groan or be unhappy. How happy can a person be when she has to do chores instead of going shopping with friends? Let youngsters feel what they feel, as long as they do what they are supposed to do.

One way to avoid getting into an unnecessary verbal struggle with a child is to stick to the Two Sentence Rule.

The Two Sentence Rule Means...

Say what you have to say in two sentences. Then stop.

Do not let yourself get drawn into an argument. Just say what needs to be said and stop. If necessary, repeat the same two sentences. Do not, however, get caught up in a dialogue that ends with your "giving up" in order to get out of the struggle. Children and teens are highly skilled at the technique of verbal struggle. When the struggle ends with their getting what they want, and you find yourself backing off from your original stance, they learn very quickly to try this same technique again and again. This doesn't make them bad kids or even a serious discipline problem. It just makes them normal human children. It is the job of the adult to make sure that the child's attempt at this time tested technique does not work. The Two Sentence Rule can help you do this.

Here is an example of the Two Sentence Rule at work:

Parent: Please get your room cleaned before you leave for the concert.

Teen: I can't. I don't have time. I'll do it as soon as I get home, before I go to bed. I promise. I had to work late, and my friend is picking me up at 7:30, and if I stop to clean my room, I'll never be ready. What difference does it make if I do it now or later? Nobody's going to see it.

Parent: I'm sorry you had to work late. Do it quickly and you'll have plenty of time to get ready. *(Two sentences.)*

Teen: But Mom, I told you...

Parent: *(Leaving the room)* Clean your room, please.

Versus

Parent: Please get your room cleaned before you leave for the concert.

Teen: I can't. I don't have time. I'll do it as soon as I get home, before I go to bed. I promise. I had to work late, and my friend is picking me up at 7:30, and if I

	stop to clean my room, I'll never be ready. What difference does it make if I do it now or later? Nobody's going to see it.
Parent:	I'll see it and it drives me crazy! I don't know how you can live this way! I'm sorry you had to work late. Do it quickly and you'll have plenty of time to get ready. I told you to do it before you went to work but you wanted to sleep. It's not my fault that you are in a crunch now! If you didn't put everything off to the last minute you wouldn't be in this crunch, and if you went to bed at a decent hour you wouldn't have to sleep to the last minute!
Teen:	It's not my fault I had to work late. The other girl didn't show up on time. I couldn't just walk out. You are always saying I should be a responsible employee and now when I am, you don't even care.
Parent:	I do care, and I'm glad you stayed at work to help out, but that does not change the fact that you should have cleaned this room yesterday. It shouldn't be in this condition in the first place, for that matter.
Teen:	I had to study yesterday. You know I have that big test on Monday. You're the one that told me to study.
Parent:	You should have studied….Yada, yada, yada…

(Many sentences and time passing....)

I'll put my money on the teenager in the second example. I think Mom is about to give in and say:

Parent: Oh, okay! Just make sure you get it
              done tomorrow.

Teenagers can usually outlast their parents in an argument. After all, they really do have more energy. I have to confess to being taught the Two Sentence Rule when my children were teenagers. It was a common occurrence for me to get caught up in a verbal struggle. It was usually about fairly inconsequential things like the example above, but nevertheless, it was exhausting. It was good for everyone when I began stopping after the second sentence. It eliminated a lot of tension and made me feel less manipulated, and it helped my teenagers learn to accept decisions sooner too. Try the Two Sentence Rule. It works.

Summary

Teaching children and teens self-control and helping them internalize those skills sometimes requires adults to repeat certain directions or commands over and over. Repetition helps the brain develop habits, especially self-control habits. Adults can use short positive phrases over and over to direct a child's or teen's behavior to what they need to do. These simple verbal cues help children develop their brain pathways, which will eventually result in positive behavior changes. Repeating the same phrases also helps them learn to say these verbal prompts to themselves, which is the beginning of developing self-control. As self-control develops, adults do not need to prompt children as often, because it has become automatic for them to do this for themselves.

Some of the short phrases that adults can use are: "Stay on task," "Focus," "Do it the first time," "Listen up," "Be kind," and "Use words." These phrases are designed to keep the focus on positive behavior. They give the brain a "to do" message rather than a "do not do" message. They tell the child to *do* something, as opposed to telling them to *stop doing* something.

It is necessary to discuss the phrases with children. Give them specific directions about what you expect them to do when you say the phrases. Ask them to agree to do this. Asking them to agree is not the same as asking them for permission to tell them what to do. The latter is not necessary, nor is it effective parenting. Asking them to agree, on the other hand, is simply a way of getting them to take responsibility for their behavior. Your responsibility is to remind them of what needs to be done, using the short phrase as a prompt. Their responsibility is to do it as soon as they hear the prompt.

Another way to help children and teens respond to verbal prompting is to use the "Two Sentence Rule." The "Two Sentence Rule" means that once a request or command has been made, then no more than two sentences should follow. Sticking with the "Two Sentence Rule" keeps adults from engaging in an argument, an unnecessary explanation or any other type of verbal struggle. Once adults make a habit of saying what needs to be said in two sentences, children will learn to respond more quickly to the directions they have been given. They will learn that the adult is not willing to engage in a debate. When using this technique it is helpful to allow children to express their emotions appropriately.

Many adults want children to immediately do what they are told and at the same time behave as if they are happy about it. Sometimes young people feel unhappy or mad when they want to do something and they feel they are not being allowed to do it. It is okay for them to feel what they feel as long as the end result is their doing what they should be doing. It is even helpful to acknowledge their *feelings* and express understanding as long as you stick to the "Two Sentence Rule" when it comes to the original request or command.

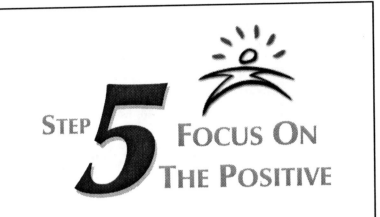

STEP 5 FOCUS ON THE POSITIVE

The value of positive thinking is almost universally accepted. Some children, especially those with serious or chronic misbehavior, can severely test a parent or teacher's ability to maintain a sincerely positive outlook. This chapter discusses the importance of acknowledging the personal character strengths and good behavior of children. This discussion will show how to help children utilize their own positive strengths to overcome or stop negative behavior.

Sometimes, during the process of teaching the fine art of self-control to children and teens, it can begin to feel as if you are just continually pointing out faults and shortcomings. Some days it can seem as if there is no time for anything else! This can lead to an impression that a particular child or teen has only faults. His or her problem behaviors somehow become the entire focus of everyone's attention.

This can happen with parents and other adults who acknowledge that their child or student must have special gifts, talents or positive characteristics. After all, don't all children have good qualities? Even the most well intentioned parent or teacher may respond to this question with, "Yes, but ...." They sincerely believe that their child or student needs to be reminded of what is wrong in order to improve or correct unacceptable behavior and develop good character. Some adults, however, have great difficulty when trying to identify *any* positive gift, talent or character strength the child has. All the adult's energy has been focused on the day-in and day-out behavior problems that the youngster has presented.

Yet, few things are more important to the process of effective discipline than keeping the focus on *positive character strengths and talents*. It is the existence and recognition of these very strengths and talents that will help children learn the new skills they must acquire in order for their behavior to change and improve. These strengths and talents will also lead them onward and into their life's work. The more their natural talents receive early positive recognition from the adults in their lives, the more likely those strengths will grow and blossom.

Difficult Behavior Takes Talent

I have always found it fascinating to observe that their natural strengths and talents can frequently get children into trouble. Actually, it takes real talent to do some of the things that children and teens do that frustrate adults the most. For instance, parents can get very frustrated with children who argue constantly. Sometimes this happens just because they have learned that a sufficient argument will usually get them what they want. Other times, it is because these children are naturally sharp witted and have a genuine talent for seeing both sides of an issue. They can present their side in a compelling manner. It is this sort of difficult behavior that can, at the same time, demonstrate some real talent.

These same children and teens can be tenacious by nature and have a difficult time giving up or admitting defeat. Tenacity, the ability to hang in there against all odds, is an admirable and valuable character trait. Some children come by it naturally. There are many such examples.[1] Even children who are prone to temper tantrums are nonetheless usually passionate about things that matter to them. Conversely, children who seem disinterested in things their parents care about are often the calm and easygoing people that most adults enjoy being around.

If you think about it, most adults have come to recognize that some of their own personal strengths, of which they are justifiably proud, have also presented problems for them from time to time. I enjoy verbal communications and get a great deal of pleasure from the training sessions I do all around the country. Some people find it almost impossible to speak before a group, yet I find it easy and enjoyable. At the same time, I have gotten in trouble a few times in my life for talking a bit too much! Some of my natural strengths can express themselves as natural weaknesses.

If adults can keep in mind that *most difficult behavior takes talent*, it will help them gain a new perspective when they experience the irritating and frustrating behavior of the children in their care. It can also prevent them from developing a negative attitude when approaching a child. They will be able to acknowledge what is right about the child, such as actually telling the child that he or

---

[1] For more information on positive strengths and difficult behavior see *Good Kids, Difficult Behavior*, Divinyi, 1997.

she is a gifted and talented person. Most of all, it will help them focus on positive expectations for the child.

Children Are Sensitive
To Adult Expectations

A child's belief that you see and believe in their positive characteristics and good intentions is one of the most powerful tools for making discipline work. When adults want their disciplinary actions to have the desired effect, the first question to ask is, "Does this young person believe and understand that I am aware of what is really right and good about them?"

Adults do not employ this tool often enough. In fact, many times, it seems to children that adults do not think there is much right about them. This can be true even for children or teens who have no doubt that their parents love them. If you ask them, "Do you think your parents love you?", the answer will be, "Yes," without any hesitation. But if you ask them, "What exactly do you think your father likes about you?" or, "What do you think your teacher likes specifically about you?", they will respond with, "I don't know … nothing I guess."

This is also true of many parents or others with children in their care. They will tell you quite readily that they love the child and that the child knows it. But if you ask them, "What is it you like about this child?", they will stumble around and have a hard time coming up with anything more than, "Well, she is a good girl and she knows I love her."

I have done this exercise with many groups of parents and teachers. Every time, numerous adults in the group need to be coached in order to identify and state something specific that is right and good about an individual child. When I am working with groups of parents and their children, it is usually easy to tell which children have probably never heard their parents say something really positive about them. This is also often true with teachers who are discussing children whose behavior has been problematic for

Discipline That Works: 5 Simple Steps

some time. They forget the child's positive traits.

One reason this happens is that adults are so focused on teaching and correcting that it is easy for them to give the child the impression they expect them to do "something wrong" at any minute. What parent hasn't reminded a child, more than once, about the last time they "goofed up?" Without meaning to, it is all too easy for adults to send the message to children that their expectations of them are quite negative.

It happens something like this:

Parent A: Did you do what I told you? You never do anything the first time I tell you! If you would just pay attention and do what you are told then I wouldn't have to be fussing all the time!

An alternative is the parent who expresses *positive* expectations:

Parent B: I'm sure you did what I told you. Focus now and get the job done. I know I can count on you.

In both examples, the assumption is that the child did not do what he was told the first time. However, the parent in the first example did a great deal more than reprove the child for not listening to directions. He told the child that he did not really *expect* the child to listen the first time, or, for that matter, the next time. Whenever there is a sentence that starts with "You never..." or "You always...," it is likely that a criticism is not far behind. Some adults even believe that it is one of their responsibilities to point out the child's faults. This is not true in general. Beyond that, unfortunately, it is not true discipline either. True discipline is aimed at teaching self-control, which requires helping children develop a positive self-concept. A constant reminder of what is wrong with a person can seriously inhibit the development of a positive self-concept.

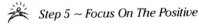

The parent in the second example kept the focus on instruction and *positive expectations*. The greatest problem with pointing out faults all the time is that it usually backfires. Why? Because we now understand that children develop their self-concept from the adults around them. Self-concept means how people see themselves. It is a foundation stone of self-control. Self-control develops best when a child has a positive self-concept or image.

People who see themselves basically as good and capable, and believe others see them that way, are much more apt to make good behavior choices. They will want to live up to the *positive* expectations that others have of them.

Expectations are powerful. People live up, or down, to the expectations others have of them. When expectations are positive, a child's or teen's self-image gets a healthy boost.

I will always remember a little eight-year-old boy who had many difficult circumstances in his life. This had resulted in chronic misbehavior as well as learning disabilities. When I first met him, he told me that he could not read. I simply nodded at this statement.

Later, I was doing an activity with him and a group of other boys. They were supposed to make posters and put them up around the room, which was our work area. I assigned different posters to different boys. When I got to this boy and told him to make a sign that said "No Kid Zone," he said, "Ms. Joyce, you know I can't read." I said, "Oh, I forgot. Why don't you go over there (where another boy was working on a similar sign) and make your sign. Just make the same letters in the same order as he does and you will have your sign. You can make your letters different sizes or different colors; just make sure they are all in the same order."

He followed directions and later came to show me the sign he made. I told him it was a good looking sign and said, "Let's go put it up." After we got the sign posted on the right door, I said, "Now tell me what it says." He said, "It says, 'No Kid Zone.'" I replied, "Look at you. You are reading. You told me you couldn't read and now I don't know what to think!" He grinned from ear to ear.

The next day, I was working with the same group. I was having the boys read aloud. Not wanting to embarrass this little guy, I just skipped past him to the next child. He looked at me with a surprised expression on his face and said, "Ms. Joyce, you know I can read." He proceeded to read aloud even though I had to help him with many words. His self-perception had changed.

Affirming that he could read changed his perception of what he believed he could do. Often the belief that we can do something is the first step in mastering a challenging task. It is important to let children and teens know that we believe in them and that we have high expectations. I often had to correct this boy's behavior. Nonetheless, I kept our interactions positive and focused on what I believed he was capable of, not on his frequent mistakes or irritating behavior. I admit that sometimes it was difficult, especially since I was working with a group of boys who all had similar difficulties with their behavior. Overall, the program that brought us all together was a great success. It succeeded largely because the intense focus of every day's work was on positive expectations and the skill building that comprise good discipline.

Praise Often

A positive self-concept can take a lifetime to develop. The foundations, however, are set in childhood. All adults in a child's life, not just parents, have an impact on a child's self-concept. That is why teachers are so important. Children spend almost as much or more time with teachers than they do with parents. How teachers interact with them can make a great deal of difference in a child's ability to develop a positive self-concept. In fact, children whose parents are not able to interact with them positively have an even greater need for any adult who can help them see themselves in a positive light. Teachers have great power to make this happen.

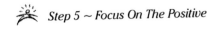

One way to do this is to acknowledge or praise a child's successes and good choices as often as possible. This is a little different from just saying something "nice" about the child. When children are praised for something they did or something special about them in particular, they are much more likely to feel pride and confidence than if they are just praised for being good.

Most children, and especially teens, are keenly aware that their behavior is not always "good." They know that they make mistakes. Sometimes they make pretty big mistakes. They are more likely to give credibility to positive comments when these comments are directed toward their personal real accomplishments rather than their general behavioral goodness.

Praise Deeds Rather Than The Person

Praising specific accomplishments can be a lengthy conversation or a simple and short comment. It just needs to refer specifically to something the child did right or well.

Examples:

Adult: I watched the way you helped that boy who was getting ready to lose his temper. You helped distract him and made him laugh. By the time he was finished talking to you he forgot how mad he was. That was a kind and clever thing to do. You ended up helping the whole class. Thanks.

or...

Adult: Hey, you were a big help in there. I appreciate it.

Both examples are directed toward the child's positive actions. Both leave the child feeling pleased with herself. Both help the child's self-concept.

Praising the child instead of the deed has a different effect.

Adult: You are so great. You saved the day in
             there. You are so sensitive to other
             people's feelings and are just such a
             good person.

In the second example, the adult means well and isn't saying anything wrong or inappropriate. He is just talking about the whole character of the child instead of a single act. Although the intention is to praise, this kind of praise can make the child feel very uncomfortable if she doesn't see herself as "great" or "sensitive" or even a "good person." This discomfort can cause the child to dismiss the praise instead of take it in.

In the first example, the child gets to feel good and proud of himself without feeling uncomfortable. He can also think about something he did that was right. Little by little, experiences such as these can have a positive impact on how children and teens see themselves. The more positive children's self-perceptions are, the more likely they are to try to act in a way that is consistent with the positive ways they see themselves. Sadly, the opposite is true as well. The more a child perceives himself as a big goof-up, the more he lives up to that perception.

Acknowledge good qualities and good choices often. The more acknowledgements the child receives, the better. It is also helpful to tell young people what you specifically like about them. It is so easy for them to think that the adults around them don't see their good qualities. Just as adults need to hear genuine words of praise and acknowledgement, children, especially teenagers, need to hear genuine and positive comments. Most adults would like to hear good words about themselves a little more often, especially from the people who matter the most to them. Children and teens are no exception.

It has been my experience that the simple act of praise and acknowledgement of good qualities is one of the most difficult things

for some adults to do. Some are even afraid, as one father confessed to me after a training class, that if he said too many positive things to his son, his son would quit trying so hard to do the right thing. In fact, the reverse is true.

Other adults are concerned that such praise and acknowledgement will not build character. There can be truth in this fear, but only if the praise is not combined with true discipline or if the praise is undeserved. When children are praised for being wonderful or even doing something wonderful, but are never chastised for unacceptable behavior, they will not develop a healthy self-concept or self-control.

A healthy self-concept, whether in adults, children or teens, includes being able to recognize and take responsibility for mistakes and poor choices. The goal is always to learn from them, and taking ownership of one's mistakes is the first step in learning from them. When parents do not allow children to take responsibility for their mistakes or poor choices, they are unintentionally limiting their child's opportunity to develop a strong character or positive self-concept.

Simple Praise Works Too

Coupling praise and simple acknowledgements with healthy discipline is the best possible combination for building the character strengths that all adults want children to develop. Praise and acknowledgement can be very simple.

The following are simple phrases of praise and acknowledgement that pack a powerful positive wallop:

> Good job!
> All right!
> I'm impressed.
> Thanks, I appreciate it.
> You did it. I knew you could.
> Good going.

There are many more. Be genuine. Be creative. Have fun with it. A playful delivery is frequently well received. Children and teens are especially impressed with adults who make them laugh. Humor is an important and valuable discipline tool.[2] Praise and acknowledgement can even be as simple as a hand signal, a thumb up, a high five, or even a wink. Anything that lets young people know you were watching and you notice them doing the right thing works!

Help Them See The Future

Acknowledging young people for doing the right thing is the best possible way to reinforce positive behavior. It also projects and reinforces your positive expectations of them. It helps you help them develop dreams and goals. Small children are not developmentally ready to think about the future much beyond the coming weekend or the next fun time they are planning. Teens, on the other hand, are expected to be future oriented, and they are when it comes to those rites of passage that most teens look forward to — such as getting a drivers license and being able to take the family car without a parent riding along. Yet, they are not always able to see themselves as grown up.

By the time teens get old enough to drive they need to be able to imagine themselves being independent and grown up. Most can imagine themselves being free from parental boundaries and restrictions. Healthy adolescents can also imagine taking care of themselves and taking responsibility for their own actions. This can be scary and confusing, since one part of them wants to hurry and grow up and another part wants to be taken care of forever! This conflict is a natural part of adolescent development and can be challenging for everyone.

There is a way adults can help adolescents navigate the tricky waters of growing from children to adults. It is to constantly remind teens that they have great potential, and you expect to see them

---

[2] See "Power Tools" in *Good Kids, Difficult Behavior*, Divinyi, 1997.

use their gifts and talents when they grow up. Be specific. Tell them exactly what you see that they do well and how the world needs their talents and gifts.

A good way to start is to say to them, "You know, what I like about you is_____, and I can see you someday as a_____." Young people need adults to have faith in them and a vision for them that they don't yet clearly see in themselves. Here are a few examples:

You know, what I like about you is:

You have an ability to stick with a problem until you solve it.

You can always make me laugh.

You have such intense feelings about things.

You can draw anything.

You can usually understand what other people are feeling.

You need things to be done right.

You stay calm no matter what is going on around you.

You think for yourself.

And I can see you someday:

Inventing things that other people think can't be done because you won't give up until you figure out how to do it.

Using your humor to help people who are having a hard time with their lives.

Being a senator or community leader trying and trying to help people less fortunate than you.

Creating the most beautiful art or designing the newest automobile.

Working with troubled kids. They'll know you understand them.

Being a great manager in almost any business you would like.

Working in a hospital emergency room because you never lose your cool and you just get the job done.

Being the leader of a group of people who have to figure out a new way to do something.

In all these examples you can give the young person a glimpse of how their talents and gifts will lead them to become successful adults. And you can show them how the world needs their particular gifts.

Too often, however, parents and adults do the opposite. It is easy to do. They say things such as:

You better learn to control your temper or you'll never be able to hold down a job.

You better get motivated because no one is going to do it for you when you leave home.

You better quit fiddling around with pictures and start learning your math. People who draw are a dime a dozen and no one is going to pay you for pictures.

You get the idea. Children and teens are sensitive to adult perceptions of them. On rare occasions, they will get mad enough at their parents or teachers and set out to prove them wrong. Usually, though, they just internalize the belief that they "will never amount to anything" and begin to live it out.

Describe The Future In Emotional Terms

There is one more thing that adds to the good effects of predicting positive futures for young people. Tell them how good it will *feel* when they use their talents in the best way to make their dreams come true. Describe how proud of themselves they will *feel*...not how proud *you* will be... but how proud *they* will be of themselves

and what a good *feeling* that is. Even in the everyday challenges of getting them to do chores and homework and other un-fun tasks, it works better to remind them of how good it will feel when it is all done and they are getting to do something they do enjoy. Instead, adults often tell youngsters that they are making themselves miserable by dragging out the inevitable. This may be true, but it is always more effective to focus on the positive.

Remember, what receives focused attention tends to expand and grow. When we let our focus rest primarily on what is wrong with a child or what needs to be corrected because we want them to be well disciplined, somehow those qualities seem to take the forefront of our attention. When we let our focus and attention move to all those things that are right, unique and lovely about this child, then those qualities seem to grow.

True discipline is *teaching* children to appreciate themselves and believe in themselves. These are cornerstones of self-discipline. Young people who see themselves in a positive way are not likely to hook up with others who devalue them or lead them in self-destructive directions. Let your focus rest on the positive and help them do likewise. This is the best part of using discipline to teach self-control.

Summary

There is no way to overstate the importance of staying focused on a child's positive behavior and natural character strengths. Many times the behaviors that cause problems and end up getting the child into trouble are the result of positive natural character strengths — the same strengths that will one day serve the child quite well. Strong willed children can become strong leaders, and mischievous children can be highly creative and inventive. Many of the finest adults I know were surely described by their parents or teachers as strong willed, stubborn or mischievous.

Looking at negative behavior as just one facet of a basically delightful young person inevitably creates positive expectations for the child or teen. Children and teens are highly sensitive to adult expectations. Without either adult or child being aware, adults send strong messages to the young ones in their care. Some messages say, "I think you are a neat kid, and I honestly expect that most of the time you will do the right thing. You'll turn out just fine." The reverse is also true. Without being aware of it, parents and adults can send unconscious but powerful messages that say, "I expect that you will screw up any minute and I can't imagine how you will ever make it in this world." Either way, children and adolescents respond to the expectations of adults. Youngsters somehow feel compelled to live up or down to those expectations.

Keep expectations positive by staying focused on the good. Praise children often and in big and little ways. Praise their deeds and not necessarily their intentions. Most children and teens are trying hard to do the right thing. Help them imagine how good it will feel to achieve goals and do the right thing. Describe their futures for them in positive emotional terms. Too often adults find themselves predicting the future in negative terms. The number of adults who can remember a parent or teacher telling them that they would never amount to anything is truly sad. All people need encouragement and lots of it. It is the best of all the simple steps that make discipline work.

Discipline That Works: 5 Simple Steps

CONCLUSION

Teaching children self-control is the goal of effective discipline. Sometimes that goal gets confused with trying to teach children that adults have control and they must be obeyed. Teaching children to obey adult rules, directions or a command is the first stage of teaching self-control. The last stage is to teach them to do the right things without adults watching and chastising. That is why true discipline is a teaching process.

Sometimes discipline gets confused with punishment. Punishment can be a tool of discipline but it cannot substitute for discipline because it only has the power, in the best circumstances, to make a child regret a mistake or inappropriate act. Punishment does not teach children and teens how to handle the same circumstances differently next time.

Teaching children the skills they need so that they can learn new behavior or figure out how to handle troublesome situations better is the crux of true discipline. One of the most significant things children and teens need to understand is how their brains work. Understanding their own brains will help them make sure that their *emotions* connect with their *thinking* before they decide to *act*. This takes time and practice. Understanding how this process works in the brain is very helpful to children when they need to get out of an emotional or impulsive mode and into a *thinking* mode.

Young people need to learn many skills in order to develop self-control. One of the first steps in self-control is self-awareness. Asking children questions about their behavior helps teach them self-awareness. Self-control develops best when they learn to pay attention to what they are doing, not just to the verbal commands of adults.

When commands and directions are necessary it helps to use short repetitive phrases rather than lectures and lengthy explanations. Adults can easily get drawn into exhausting dialogues with children and especially teens. Adults need to remember to make a conscious effort to limit the number of words and phrases they use to tell a child or teen what they need to do or not do. The best bet is to keep the directions and commands as short as possible.

It is also important for adults to focus on the strengths and natural gifts of the young people in their care. Effective discipline does not require constant criticism, but it can seem that way at times. Adults need to take special care to talk to children and teens about what is good and right about them, and how those good qualities will serve them well as young adults.

The most important and valuable job in the world is to help children develop a strong and positive sense of themselves. This in turn helps them manage their own behavior well. It is a challenging assignment for any adult who decides to participate. It is also the most rewarding and gratifying goal a person can achieve.

Children and teens can be wonderfully enjoyable. Using the 5 Simple Steps for Discipline That Works will help you enjoy your daily interactions with children, while helping them grow and mature in the healthiest way possible.

Recommended Reading

Barkley, Russell A. *Defiant Children: A Clinician's Manual for Parents Training*. New York: The Guilford Press, 1987.

De Becker, Gavin. *Protecting the Gift: Keeping Children and Teenagers Safe (And Parents Sane)*. New York: Dell Books, 2000.

Divinyi, Joyce E. Storytelling: An Enjoyable and Effective Therapeutic Tool. *Contemporary Family Therapy, An International Journal*, 1995.

Dobson, James C. *Hide or Seek*. Grand Rapids, MI: Ravell, 1974.

Faber, Adele, Mazlish, Elaine et al. *How To Talk So Kids Can Learn*. Simon & Schuster Audio Division, 1995. (Audio Cassette)

Ginott, Haim G. *Between Parent and Child*. New York: Avon Books, 1965.

Glenn, H. Stephen and Nelsen, Jane. *Raising Self-Reliant Children in a Self-Indulgent World*. Rocklin, CA: Prima Publishing and Communications, 1989.

Glenn, H. Stephen and Nelsen, Jane. *Time Out — Abuses and Effective Uses*. Fair Oaks, CA: Sunrise Press, 1991.

Goleman, Daniel. *Emotional Intelligence*. New York: Bantam Books, 1995.

Greene, Ross W. *The Explosive Child: A New Approach for Understanding and Parenting Easily Frustrated, Chronically Inflexible Children.* New York: HarperCollins, 2001.

Hartmann, Thom et al. *Attention Deficit Disorder: A Different Perception.* Lancaster, PA: Underwood-Miller, 1993.

Kondracki, Linda. *All My Feelings Are Okay (Confident Kids: Guides for Growing a Healthy Family).* Grand Rapids, MI: Fleming H. Revell (A Division of Baker Book House Co), 1993.

Koplewicz, Harold S. *It's Nobody's Fault: New Hope and Help for Difficult Children and Their Parents.* New York: Times Books, 1996.

Magid, Ken and McKelvey, Carole A. *High Risk: Children Without a Conscience.* Golden, CO: M&M Publishing Co., 1987.

Thompson, George J. and Jenkins, Jerry B. *Verbal Judo — The Gentle Art of Persuasion.* New York: William Morrow and Company, Inc., 1993.

Tobin, L. *What Do You Do With a Child Like This? Inside the Lives of Troubled Children.* Duluth, MN: Whole Person Associates, 1991.

Tobin, L. *62 Ways to Create Change in the Lives of Troubled Children.* Duluth, MN: Whole Person Associates, 1991.

Waliszewski, Bob and Melchisedeck, Jerry. *Bringing Out the Worst in Us. Focus on the Family Culture Report. The Frightening Truth About Violence, The Media and Our Youth.* To obtain a copy of this report you may call Focus on the Family at 1-800-A-FAMILY.

Also recommended: All the Calvin and Hobbes books, by Bill Watterson, to remind you to keep your sense of humor when dealing with difficult children...besides, Calvin has the CAN DO and I COUNT attitudes down pat.

Joyce Divinyi, M.S., L.P.C.

Psychotherapist, Author, Lecturer

"What were you thinking of?" is the question most frequently heard from adults trying their best to deal with difficult and unacceptable behavior in children. Joyce Divinyi's expertise in human behavior provides the foundation for her informative, engaging and entertaining presentations in which she helps audiences from all walks of life find the answer to this troubling and frustrating question.

Ms. Divinyi has extensive experience working with troubled children and teens in a variety of settings, including schools, private practice counseling, in-patient and out-patient psychiatric facilities and residential treatment programs.

Ms. Divinyi has an Atlanta-based private practice in individual and family therapy and is the owner of The Human Connection, a company dedicated to improving people to people interaction. She has trained in schools, churches, juvenile court systems and treatment centers throughout the United States. She has two grown daughters and lives and works in Peachtree City, Georgia.

For more information, visit our website at
www.thehumanconnection.net

For information about the author, other publications, or training programs, please visit our website.

www.thehumanconnection.net

Books:

Good Kids, Difficult Behavior: A Guide to What Works and What Doesn't

The ABCs Workbook: Creating a Behavior Change Plan That Works

Audiotapes:

Successful Strategies for Dealing with Difficult Students

Safe and Effective Strategies for Defusing Hostile Students

Motivating the Unmotivated Student

Communicating Effectively with Difficult Parents

Video Tape:

Creating Safety: How to Identify and Respond to the Potentially Dangerous Student

The Human Connection
Toll Free: 1-888-460-8022 or
770-631-8264
Fax: 770-486-1609

649.64   Divinyi, Joyce
DIVINYI   Discipline that works

R0102222934

NORTHSIDE

ATLANTA-FULTON COUNTY LIBRARY

MAR   2011